Tech Tools for Improving Student Literacy

Technology isn't just fun to use in the classroom; it can also make real improvements in students' literacy development. In this book, authors Hilarie Davis and Bradford Davey show you how and why to use tech tools to help enhance the teaching of reading, writing, speaking, listening, and viewing. These tools can be used in English/Language Arts and across the subject areas to promote literacy throughout your school.

Special Features:

- Practical classroom examples from a variety of content areas
- Connections to specific Common Core State Standards
- "Using the Technology" boxes with step-by-step guidance
- Screenshots that show how the tools work
- Strategies to help you use the tools effectively with students

Bradford Davey is Senior Researcher at Technology for Learning Consortium, Inc.

Hilarie Davis is President and CEO of Technology for Learning Consortium, Inc.

D1529815

Tech Tools for Improving Student Literacy

Bradford Davey and Hilarie Davis

Routledge
Taylor & Francis Group

NEW YORK AND LONDON

First published 2014
by Routledge
711 Third Avenue, New York, NY 10017

and by Routledge
2 Park Square, Milton Park, Abingdon, Oxon, OX14 4RN

Routledge is an imprint of the Taylor & Francis Group, an informa business

© 2014 Taylor & Francis

The rights of Bradford Davey and Hilarie Davis to be identified as authors of this work has been asserted by them in accordance with sections 77 and 78 of the Copyright, Designs and Patents Act 1988.

Trademark notice: Product or corporate names may be trademarks or registered trademarks, and are used only for identification and explanation without intent to infringe.

Library of Congress Cataloging-in-Publication Data

Davis, Hilarie.
   Tech tools for improving student literacy / Hilarie Davis, Bradford Davey.
      pages cm
   Includes bibliographical references.
 1. Educational technology. 2. Literacy. I. Davey, Bradford. II. Title.
LB1028.3.D285   2014
371.33—dc23   2013034348

ISBN: 978-0-415-73471-4 (hbk)
ISBN: 978-0-415-73314-4 (pbk)
ISBN: 978-1-315-81979-2 (ebk)

Typeset in Optima
by Apex CoVantage, LLC

Printed and bound in the United States of America by Publishers Graphics,
LLC on sustainably sourced paper.

Contents

Meet the Authors

Following a long and winding path, **Bradford Davey** has found his calling working with the blending of emerging technologies and learning. Brad is an experienced classroom teacher who taught high school and middle school science and mathematics for 10 years. During that time, he was able to develop his understanding for and appreciation of the learning process, how it differs for every individual, and the importance of helping learners find their passion to promote their own learning and growth. Brad began his journey as a medical researcher believing he was bound for medical school. While working in the lab, he had the opportunity to teach other laboratory technicians and students and fell in love with teaching, eventually transitioning into teaching science in the classroom.

While teaching in the classroom and serving as Science Department Head, Brad met Hilarie. They began their relationship sharing their love for each other and their work. After a year, they combined their efforts and started working together full time. To better understand the complex and dynamic world of educational technology, Brad went back to school to earn his Master's from Pepperdine University in Educational Technology and Leadership. He has used his degree to help groups such as NASA and NOAA develop cutting-edge learning environments. Brad also earned his doctorate in learning technologies from Pepperdine University, studying the development of an online community of practice for NASA and determining factors of community design and usage to produce community-knowledge building and growth. Brad continues to look for innovative ways of leveraging existing technologies in powerful ways for learning. Brad has also worked to capture participant learning through video and has been successful in using videos he and Hilarie have developed as evidence of learning outcomes.

Hilarie Davis became a reading specialist because she was intrigued with the complexity of learning language. As a philosophy undergraduate major at SUNY Brockport, she focused on epistemology, or how people learn. Recognizing that reading is one of the most important skills that children learn, she pursued a master's degree in Reading before working in a Title IV-C reading program for eighth graders who could not read. By the end of the year, they all scored at the sixth-grade level or higher on a standardized test of reading. That "videographics" program had students research, plan, and make their own videos so their misconceptions or missing bits about language were revealed and could be taught. She was also trained in holistic writing scoring in the first wave of teachers in New York State. For her doctoral work at the University of Rochester,

Hilarie pursued ideas in development, learning, and instruction, focusing on underachievement and competence.

As Hilarie went on to become a Director of Curriculum, she never forgot about the motivation of the videographics students and the focused instruction she was able to do with them because of pinpoint diagnosis and their need to know. In that role, she focused on developing teachers' use of holistic scoring for diagnosis and instruction, reading across the content areas, and use of rich text and the arts in literacy. As Vice President of Curriculum and Instruction for Optical Data Corporation, she shepherded the development and implementation of the first multimedia program to compete successfully with elementary science textbooks. The program was based on a Circle of Learning that used images, hands-on activities, and concept mapping to develop concepts before reading science texts and fictional stories about science concepts. As a researcher at the federally funded Lab at Brown University, Hilarie studied literacy programs and how they are developed and sustained, producing a documentary on District #2 in New York City. Since then, Hilarie has worked on curriculum development as well as evaluations of large-scale programs for NASA and the National Oceanic and Atmospheric Administration (NOAA), establishing feedback loops and examining effects over time.

Together, Hilarie Davis, President and CEO of Technology for Learning Consortium Inc., and her husband and partner Bradford Davey, Senior Researcher and Subject Matter Expert, specialize in working with organizations and projects to develop, support, and evaluate student-centered learning environments; develop curriculum; and bridge the gap between learning and technology. When they are not traveling for work, Hilarie and Brad live in Rhode Island where they love to sail and swim as much as possible. During the winter, they can often be found on the ski slopes of Colorado enjoying powder skiing after big storms.

Preface

Science and technology multiply around us. To an increasing extent they dictate the languages in which we speak and think. Either we use those languages, or we remain mute.
—J. G. Ballard, author of *Empire of the Sun* and *The Kindness of Women*

The power of language has survived the onslaught of technology for centuries, in spite of dire predictions to the contrary. When writing was introduced in ancient Greece, there were fears that oration, with its requirements for memory and critical thinking, would be lost. When the printing press was invented, it was predicted that people would stop writing by hand. As the Internet has developed, concerns have been raised that people will stop communicating face to face and that writing will become corrupted into a form of shorthand.

In fact, not only have these fears about the demise of language in one form or another not been realized but language has thrived in each of these new technological environments. Critical thinking was enhanced with the creation of "dialogues" in writing. People were inspired to write more as they read more books, which became available from the printing press for the first time in great numbers. Instead of making language less important, the access to a wide audience has made people write more and better because it will be read on the Internet.

In these examples (and there are many others), each new technology has been met with a sense of resignation by many: "I guess it's inevitable (sigh)." But in each case, a few people have latched onto the technologies, immersed themselves in them, and talked about what they were doing with others. Very soon after a period in which these early adopters struggled with the technologies and peer pressure not to use them, others came around, and then the growth was exponential.

This book is about connecting the new and the old, celebrating the power and magic of language with interesting technology tools. Since language is at the core of teaching and learning, we provide examples of how technology can be used in different subject areas for reading and writing, speaking and listening, and viewing and producing.

In each case, we introduce the reasons you might want to use technology in terms of the potential it holds for enhancing and extending the use of language. Then we provide a range of options that you might latch onto—some easy and cheap, others more complicated and requiring more sophisticated technologies. We hope one or more of these will catch your fancy and suit the conditions that you work in so you can begin to experiment. **We always recommend several**

tools so that, even if some may no longer be available, you can get the idea for how to use the technology with whatever tool is available at the time.

No matter what you teach, you can use technology to enhance the use of language. Advances in technology have created new ways to communicate; challenges to how we think; and access to people, ideas, and media. For our students, the "digital natives" technology is the new way home. It is how they become literate and learn to value the power of language.

The book discusses the use of technology from a literacy development perspective. It answers the question, "What is the value of this technology for literacy development?" By presenting the technologies within the literacy goals of reading and writing, speaking and listening, and viewing and producing, the use of the tools is focused on literacy development rather than using technology for technology's sake.

Introduction and How to Use this Book

Each section has some key ideas. We list them to give you an overview and sneak preview. We'll repeat them at the beginning of each section too. By knowing what we're thinking, you can also dive into whatever seems interesting to you.

Section I: Reading and Writing

Language exerts hidden power, like a moon on the tides.

—Rita Mae Brown

Key ideas

- Reading and writing are reciprocal.
- Technology aids reading through read-alongs; connecting to geography; providing aids for vocabulary and other concepts through links, access to reviews, and annotations; note-taking for reading nonfiction, and finding back stories and context.
- Technology supports writing through word processing, templates for different kinds of writing (presentation tools, templates in Word), outlining (*Inspiration*), publishing (printing, blogs), group writing (wikis), and publishing for others to read.

Section II: Speaking and Listening

The simple lesson teachers seem to forget is that learning to communicate is learning to think.

—Terry Robert and Laura Billings, 2009

Key ideas

- Speaking and listening are how we communicate first and most often, even after we learn to read and write.
- Speaking allows some students to present their ideas more completely and fluently than writing.

- Audio recording of speech allows the listener to hear all of the aspects of speech and the speaker to capture it for themselves to review and improve.

- Audio-captured speeches or conversations can become the basis for reading and writing.

- Speaking and listening are media for critical thinking.

- Technology tools for speaking and listening support individual differences in learning by offering multiple methods of presentation, expression, and engagement.

- Listening to lyrics can involve students in understanding characters, themes, and cultures.

- Listening to recorded stories or texts engages some students better than reading.

- Listening to others gives students a opportunity to connect, engage, and collaborate.

- Creating recordings for sharing with a wider audience can encourage students to refine their ideas and expression.

Section III: Viewing and Producing

Without image, thinking is impossible.

—Aristotle

Key ideas

- Today's learners are immersed in a very visually stimulating media world.

- Images are highly engaging and convey large amounts of information, perhaps providing the experience closest to daily life.

- Children between the ages of 8 and 18 are exposed to an average of 10 hours of media daily (TV, music, computers, and video games), with two-thirds having a TV in their bedroom.

- Visual literacy standards have evolved to help teachers direct student learning and have been adopted by 49 states.

- Proficiency in 21st-century visual literacy includes developing skills using the tools of technology—designing and sharing information; managing, analyzing, and synthesizing multiple streams of simultaneous information; and creating, critiquing, analyzing, and evaluating multimedia tasks.

- Proficiency in visual literacy also includes understanding how and why media messages are constructed, examining how individuals interpret messages differently, and understanding how media can influence beliefs and behaviors.

- Producing visual material is a natural continuation of mastering understanding of visual imagery.

Section IV: Multi-Literacies (multimodal)

A computer does not substitute for judgment any more than a pencil substitutes for literacy.

—Robert McNamara

Key ideas

● Project-based learning can be used as a powerful learning tool in conjunction with 21st-century technologies.

● Students learn by researching, collecting data, collaborating with their peers, being mentored, and exploring.

● There are many online projects sites that can help facilitate project-based learning in the classroom.

● Having work reviewed by our peers is a powerful learning tool and intensifies learning.

● Students can publish their ideas for their peers through blogging, sharing documents, developing slide shows and video, writing articles, and utilizing local media.

● Students learn from other students by paying attention, retaining what they see, reproducing behaviors, and gaining the motivation to succeed.

● Keeping up with technology can be a big challenge for any educator—building a personal learning network will help.

Reading and Writing

Language exerts hidden power, like a moon on the tides.
　　　　　—Rita Mae Brown (*Starting From Scratch*, 1988. U.S. author and social activist)

Key ideas

● Reading and writing are reciprocal.

● Technology aids reading through read-alongs; connecting to geography; providing aids for vocabulary and other concepts through links, access to reviews, and annotations; note-taking for reading nonfiction, and finding back stories and context.

● Technology supports writing through word processing, templates for different kinds of writing (presentation tools, templates in Word), outlining (*Inspiration*), publishing (printing, blogs), group writing (wikis), and publishing for others to read.

Reading and writing are reciprocal processes. Readers love or hate, understand or are baffled by, appreciate or reject writers' work. Writers consciously choose their audiences of readers, using language to engage their hoped-for readers in what they create. Perhaps most importantly, reading can help improve one's writing, and writing can increase appreciation for the writing of others.

Why insinuate technology between the reader and text? Between the writer and text? Because technology tools aid readers in better understanding and interpreting the writing of others, and in producing their own texts. Technology can help them organize their thoughts, make connections, and communicate their ideas through multiple media. And in the end, learning can be made much easier.

In this section, we present some tried-and-true reading and writing strategies with technology enhancements, along with some strategies that are only possible with technology.

Research on Technology for Reading and Writing

Reading

There are many influences on reading comprehension. Technology has changed the way learners relate to information and, in doing so, changed the way they read. Traditionally, the writer guides the reader along and shapes comprehension based on the order of information and events. With the emergence of hypertext and the Internet, authors have given over much of that control to the reader. Reading from online material, readers become the determiner of the reading sequences (McNabb, 2005) by following their interests and, in doing so, shaping their comprehension. Unfortunately, online reading often becomes an independent event because classroom teachers prefer to leave online instruction to the technology teacher or to create independent assignments utilizing the Internet, while the technology teacher focuses on literacy skills rather than guiding students in content-area reading on the Internet (McNabb, 2005).

In addition to influencing reading comprehension, technology also affects reading strategies and the contextual information the reader can access. Reading strategies are the "mental operations involved when readers approach a text effectively and make sense of what they read" (Barnett, 1998, p. 1) and include determining word meaning and predicting, inferring, and distinguishing between main ideas and supporting details. Prereading activities such as brainstorming help readers develop successful strategies and lead to greater comprehension (Barnett, 1998). Contextual information can affect a reader's comprehension, interest, and motivation (Sun et al., 2005), and includes knowing about the author's background, background of the setting for the text, and learning historical information about when the story was written or takes place. Technology-enhanced reading materials allow the reader greater access to contextual information through hyperlinks, Internet searches, source materials, and additional readings (Loretta, 2002; Marino, 2008).

Different reading strategies also emerge from the incorporation of technology with reading. Note-taking, an external strategy, is essential for critical reading and enhances reader comprehension (Kobayashi, 2007) and has been linked to test performance (Peverly et al., 2007). Taking notes represents a form of external storage of information, and learners' ability to effectively access their notes reveals much about their comprehension of the material. Traditionally, notes are written down in a 'notebook' and are used to study from at a later date. The access to notes in a notebook is mostly linear, leaving the learner to reread notes and turning them into an abbreviated version of the original text, along with their own reactions and questions. Notes taken electronically can have a much different form. Good note-takers both produce high-quality written notes and relate the topics within the notes to other pieces of important information. By encoding notes in this way, the new material is integrated with prior knowledge and internalized (Kiewra, 1989). Relationships within electronic notes can take the form of links, images, quoted passages, and videos, enhancing the learners' encoding and ultimately their comprehension.

Writing

Like it or not, a piece of writing usually improves with revisions. As early as 1984, Newman identified the role of word processing in improving writing by encouraging the writer to experiment with many facets of the writing process at the same time. Writers can keep a thought in their heads while they play with the language on the screen with which they are trying to represent that thought or image. Ten years later, an ERIC publication on word processing by Simic (1994) pointed out that the word processor benefits both the novice and the more experienced writer. "Even a beginner can use the delete, strikeover, and insert functions to make simple changes. Later, with a brief period of practice, more complex changes, such as changing the order of the sections in a paper or adding passages written in another draft, can be made" (p. 1). No more copying, recopying, and deciphering notes. The mechanical part of editing becomes easy with a word processor, so the writer can play with the words and ideas until the "language exerts its hidden power."

A meta-analysis of experimental and quasi-experimental studies of effective writing instruction produced for the Carnegie Corporation (Graham & Perin, 2007a) identified 11 elements found to be effective in teaching adolescents to write well and to use writing as a way to learn. Word processing was found to have a moderate effect size of .51 in general, which jumped to .70 when only low-achieving writers were considered. Students report that the lack of keyboarding skills can diminish the benefits of word processing, since hunting and pecking can interfere with thinking (Dalton & Hannafin, 1987). One must free the fingers to free the mind.

When most of us were in school, assignments were given; we then brainstormed, outlined, drafted, and refined our work, ultimately handing it in to our teacher. If we were lucky, we got a good grade. If we got a good grade, we might bring it home for our parents to read. Our teachers and parents represented our primary audiences and determiners of the worthiness of our work (Karchmer, 2001). More authentic writing experiences have replaced that. Now students solve problems, do their own investigations, and create original work that has the potential to reach a much wider audience because of its value and the ability to post it online. However, just as we needed to be aware of our teachers and parents as the audiences we were writing for, now students need to think about this larger, broader audience in their writing (Calkins, 1994). Although the publishing may be informal, the writer and his or her writing may have an even greater impact than ever before.

While writing for a broader audience about meaningful topics has a profound effect on writers, it also creates a more complex writing environment where mentoring can play an important role (Sanchez & Harris, 1996). Electronic mentoring relationships offer greater flexibility in the type of relationship formed and how it is utilized (Bierema & Merriam, 2002), while still offering the traditional benefits of a mentoring relationship: improved self-esteem; improved academic skills; and support for new behaviors, attitudes, and ambitions (Guetzloe, 1997). A large group of electronic mentoring programs focused on K–12 learners have been well studied and are currently available, ranging from peer-to-peer mentoring game environments to a professional–student relationship (Bennett, 1997), and can be found listed at the National School Network Telementoring & Mentor Center.

Appearing throughout the coming chapters on reading and writing are the corresponding Common Core State Standards (CCSS) for Reading and Writing (corestandards.org). While we try to connect CCSS to the writing and examples, there are likely more ties to the text than we have indicated. We identify these connections to help you recognize how developing a technology-rich learning environment does not preclude you from meeting the requirements of your school or district for integrating local, state, and national standards into your curriculum. A CCSS connection is listed with each activity throughout the book. The CCSS we have made connections to in this section are as follows:

Reading

- Key Ideas and details
    - Read closely to determine what the text says explicitly and to make logical inferences from it; cite specific textual evidence when writing or speaking to support conclusions drawn from the text.

- ○ Determine central ideas or themes of a text and analyze their development; summarize the key supporting details and ideas.
- ○ Analyze how and why individuals, events, and ideas develop and interact over the course of a text.
- Craft and Structure
  - ○ Interpret words and phrases as they are used in a text, including determining technical, connotative, and figurative meanings, and analyze how specific word choices shape meaning or tone.
  - ○ Analyze the structure of texts, including how specific sentences, paragraphs, and larger portions of the text (e.g., a section, chapter, scene, or stanza) relate to each other and the whole.
  - ○ Assess how point of view or purpose shapes the content and style of a text.
- Integration of Knowledge and Ideas
  - ○ Integrate and evaluate content presented in diverse formats and media, including visually and quantitatively, as well as in words.
  - ○ Delineate and evaluate the argument and specific claims in a text, including the validity of the reasoning as well as the relevance and sufficiency of the evidence.
  - ○ Analyze how two or more texts address similar themes or topics in order to build knowledge or to compare the approaches the authors take.
- Range of Reading and Level of Text Complexity
  - ○ Read and comprehend complex literary and informational texts independently and proficiently.

Writing

- Text Types and Purposes
  - ○ Write arguments to support claims in an analysis of substantive topics or texts, using valid reasoning and relevant and sufficient evidence.
  - ○ Write informative/explanatory texts to examine and convey complex ideas and information clearly and accurately through the effective selection, organization, and analysis of content.
  - ○ Write narratives to develop real or imagined experiences or events using effective technique, well-chosen details, and well-structured event sequences.
- Production and Distribution of Writing
  - ○ Produce clear and coherent writing in which the development, organization, and style are appropriate to task, purpose, and audience.
  - ○ Develop and strengthen writing as needed by planning, revising, editing, rewriting, or trying a new approach.
  - ○ Use technology, including the Internet, to produce and publish writing and to interact and collaborate with others.

- Research to Build and Present Knowledge
  - Conduct short as well as more sustained research projects based on focused questions, demonstrating understanding of the subject under investigation.
  - Gather relevant information from multiple print and digital sources, assess the credibility and accuracy of each source, and integrate the information while avoiding plagiarism.
  - Draw evidence from literary or informational texts to support analysis, reflection, and research.
- Range of Writing
  - Write routinely over extended time frames (time for research, reflection, and revision) and shorter time frames (a single sitting or a day or two) for a range of tasks, purposes, and audiences.

For updated standards and more information, visit the Common Core State Standards Initiative (www.corestandards.org).

1 | Technology Tools for Reading

What does it take to unlock meaning in text? This task begins with thinking. Readers often need preparation *before* reading to help them understand the text. That preparation is usually some combination of becoming interested, thinking about what there is to know, understanding how the text is structured, and setting a purpose. This is followed by actively reading and note-taking to process the text and check their own understanding as they go. Such strategies as SQ3R, the use of hypertext, DRTA, Reciprocal Teaching, and double-entry journals, which are described later, translate well from paper to digital and even have some advantages in the digital environment. In addition, book reviews and information about the author, historical period, or setting are more easily located on the Internet and enrich students' understanding of the text than through traditional methods. These materials can lead into reading, accompany the reader along the way, or provide interesting side trips.

CCSS Connection

- Read closely to determine what the text says explicitly and to make logical inferences from it.
- Determine central ideas or themes of a text and analyze their development; summarize the key supporting details and ideas.
- Analyze how and why individuals, events, and ideas develop and interact over the course of a text.

Survey, Question, Read, Recite, Review (SQ3R) is a reading comprehension method that can help students build a framework to understand a text. This method can be helpful to students because it helps readers develop a mental framework in which to fit what they read. SQ3R is primarily used with textbook reading and assignments, although it does have other applications with any expository text. A related strategy is **Directed Reading/Thinking Activity** (DRTA), which encourages students to be active and thoughtful readers by activating their prior knowledge. DRTA helps students learn to monitor their understanding as they read and strengthen their reading and critical thinking skills. Using DRTA can be helpful because most students require explicit instruction when it comes to reading comprehension strategies. Another strategy is **Reciprocal Teaching,** an instructional activity that puts the student into the role of teacher in small-group reading sessions and was originally developed to help scaffold struggling readers. The teacher first models and then helps students learn to guide the group discussion using summarizing, question gathering, clarifying, and predicting. **Double-entry journals** enable students to record their responses to text as they read. Journaling in this way gives students the opportunity to express their thoughts and ideas as they actively engage in reading. Double-entry journals can be used with most student age groups but often help students new to an idea or text formulate an opinion and ideas as they explore, upping their engagement, interest, and success in understanding the text.

SQ3R Goes Digital

The classic Survey, Question, Read, Recite, and Review strategy (SQ3R; shown in Figure 1.1; Robinson, 1941) is enhanced in a digital environment. First, readers look over (*Survey*) the text to see how it is structured, how long it is, and what the main ideas are (from the headings), as well as to get a general feel for the language of the text. Next, they ask *Questions* they think they can answer from reading. They may have their own questions, turn the headings into questions, or develop other questions as they survey the text. As they turn to *Reading*, they try to answer their own questions and pose additional questions that they find the text answers to as they go. They use the *knowledge of the structure* from their surveying, and the *purpose of the text* from the questions, to understand what the author is trying to get across in the text. As they read, they *Recite* what they are learning. While "recite" is an old-fashioned word, its meaning of "saying without looking" aptly captures what the reader needs to do to both check on her own understanding as she is reading and to remember what she reads. By asking her own questions before reading, the reader has a real and personal reason for reading—to answer those questions she posed. The simple *process of asking the questions creates the need to find answers*. In the *Review* step, the reader realizes what she has not yet captured or does not know when she tries to get the whole picture just from the study guide she has created.

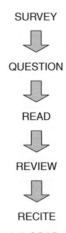

Figure 1.1 SQ3R strategy

How Can Technology Support This Process?

With printed text, whether fiction or nonfiction, the reader can use several different technologies with the SQ3R process. Using a word processor immediately enhances the process because the "survey" becomes the outline for a personal study guide, punctuated with questions and answered through reading. This guide is the crib sheet for checking on what is remembered "without looking" and the review tool for checking understanding of the whole text. The guide is constructed as the reader fills in what she understands about each section or chapter. While this can be done on paper, it is easier and more fluid when the outline can be filled in, expanded with new ideas and information, and rearranged online. The guide reveals what the reader does and doesn't understand through the lack of answers for some questions or its incomplete or unsatisfying answers, sending her back into the text. Moreover, constructing the guide is an active process that engages the reader in constantly thinking about the text and her own understanding.

The student-constructed overview, developed from surveying the text and followed by thinking about the questions she would expect to have answered, makes the *process individual and personal*, unlike teacher-provided study guides. We have seen SQ3R take on some very interesting forms in the digital classroom. One of particular interest had students using a shared Google Doc to record their reactions and thoughts about Robert Frost's poem "The Road Less Taken." The teacher posted the poem, stanza by stanza. Then students wrote their reflections, questions, and thoughts in the Google Doc. For example, one student wrote, "It's difficult to make a choice when you don't really know what that choice will lead to." Another questioned, "Why wonder when you don't have enough information to make a decision?" Students were able to see what the others thought, the questions they had, and what they had learned from reading and then shared what they thought about what they read. Together, the class utilized technology to make their thinking visible and then available for further discussion. Since everyone was adding their ideas, the discussion was much richer. The process liberated students to have their own interpretation, since there were clearly many ways to interpret and react to the poem.

Although widely used and adapted since the 1940s, SQ3R has been criticized by some as an unproven strategy (Feldt, Byme, & Bral, 1996; Lipson & Wixson, 2003; Schlozman & Schlozman, 2000). Technology can also help mitigate the criticism that assigning students to use the strategy does not inherently prepare them to use it. They may need models and instruction, particularly when transitioning from an emphasis on narrative to expository text in middle school. The teacher can post templates and models in a common web space. By having students also post their notes in this common space as they read, each student can check her own understanding against other students' understanding of the same reading. Consider VoiceThread (VoiceThread. com) as a technology tool. With VoiceThread, you can post reading passages and you and your students can post comments using text and voice. They can also get additional review of the key ideas by reading the questions and notes of other students. You can see where they need strategy instruction and communicate with them individually or do mini-lessons based on gaps in the students' guides. This facilitates a more "guided design" (Feldt et al., 1996) in which the student learns how to check her own use of the strategy and self-correct. For example, you can post a statement about a text in a VoiceThread entry and ask students to survey the text, ask questions, and read it to agree or disagree with that statement. After introducing 3Q3R, a teacher posted this statement: "Lincoln was less interested in freeing the slaves than keeping the country together." Students worked in groups to read and then discuss passages selected from Lincoln's diary and his speeches, as well as some biographer's ideas. Together they decided whether they agreed or disagreed with the statement based on evidence in what they read. One person from the group posted to VoiceThread expressing the group's ideas. The other group members listened to all of the VoiceThreads and discussed the issues in class.

Reading Digital Text

With digital text, a note-taking and reflection strategy like SQ3R has even more power and versatility. Using the copy, drag, and drop functions, headings can move from the Internet, Word documents, or PDF files to a personal study guide page, where they can be transformed from phrases to questions, quoted, paraphrased, or questioned. Using a visual mapping tool such as *Inspiration*, headings can be dropped into bubbles, and connections can be made as the text is processed. Or an outline can be created and converted to a diagram so connecting lines can be added later as a review tool. With two screens open, the reader can take notes and see them side by side with the text. Readers can create their own marking system that lets them edit the text directly—writing in questions, circling key ideas, and drawing lines to make connections. Many tablets allow users to write on the text directly, and as more of this type of technology becomes available, we will likely see tablets becoming more popular in the classroom.

A nice activity for getting started with digital textbooks and online books has students taking on a virtual exploration. To develop a simple text exploration, take students through a book looking for clues, gathering facts, and collecting photos in a visual map. For example, using a description of the history of flight, students can create their own individual maps tracing where the Wright brothers started in Ohio to their trip to Kitty Hawk, complete with dates and events.

A listing of books online can be found at a site like "Online Books" at http://onlinebooks. library.upenn.edu. Students can download books that are free and readable. This site also points to archives of online texts and interesting categories of online books (women writers, banned books, and prize-winning books). Banned books provide a good cross-curricular connection between literature and history. The site also provides ideas and resources to encourage the publication of online books. Other sites for online books include www.pagebypagebooks.com/, www.bartleby.com/, www.questia.com/, www.magickeys.com/books/, and www.gutenberg. org/catalog/.

Hypertext Creates Flexibility

Some students may prefer using a slide show tool such as Keynote for the Mac or PowerPoint for their notes and reflections. The advantage of a hypertext tool is that the slides or pages can be moved around (think about the original *HyperCard* with its metaphor of a stack of cards). Imagine having a series of pages with questions, visuals, and notes on key points and audio files for each of several sources. Each slide of the PowerPoint is a 'card' containing the pertinent information. Review slide shows can incorporate all the slides organized by concept, question, or source or some of the slides about one topic. Synthesizing questions can be inserted to organize the slides. Slide collections from different sources can be merged. Each student in a group can create a slide show on one source and then contribute to the combined slide show. Creating slides to share encourages students to develop a thorough understanding of the content and provides the opportunity to compare ideas from different sources, invoking higher levels of comprehension and synthesis.

For example, in a study of volcanoes, students are challenged to predict the next volcanic eruption in the United States. They are divided into small groups, with each group studying a different volcano in the Northwest, including its history, type, current state, monitoring data that are available, and other questions they feel that they need to answer to predict an eruption. Each group creates "slides" for each key point and then makes some slides about what it learned about predicting volcanic eruptions in general. One person from each group works on a team putting the slides from all the groups together in a prediction slide show first reviewed by the small groups and then by the whole class. The original research by the small groups is then blended back into the "prediction" slide show as examples.

Directed Reading/Thinking Activity (DRTA)

Another strategy for active reading is Directed Reading/Thinking Activity (DRTA), developed by Russell G. Stauffer (1969; shown in Figure 1.2). It can be either teacher facilitated or used independently: Students read the title, scan the pictures and text, and list ideas that come to mind. Based on this knowledge, they make predictions about what they will read about in the text, being sure to say what they based their predictions on. After reading a section, students stop and revise or confirm their predictions, stating the evidence they found in the text. Valmont (2003) suggests that teachers prepare for teacher-directed DRTAs using electronic texts by doing screen

Examine Evidence

Make Predictions

Find Proof

Stay Open to New Evidence

Make Decisions

Figure 1.2 DRTA model

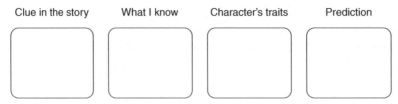

| Clue in the story | What I know | Character's traits | Prediction |

Figure 1.3 Template to help students use DRTA

captures or by bookmarking the beginning pages of a segment to prompt students to make predictions, followed by having students read for evidence to support their predictions or revise them. This same exercise translates well to online articles.

CCSS Connection

- Determine central ideas or themes of a text and analyze their development; summarize the key supporting details and ideas.

Templates can help student use DRTA as an independent tool (see Figure 1.3). For example, Roanoke County Public Schools has a downloadable slide show for students on how to make predictions using clues from the story and what the reader already knows. It offers a visual tool for thinking "like a detective" while reading (adapted from www.rcs.k12.va.us/pfes/third%20grade/reading%20sem%201%20theme%202/balto/make%20predictions.ppt). What makes DRTA such a powerful learning tool is that it encourages students to be active and thoughtful readers, while activating their prior knowledge.

Webspaces for Note-Taking and Reflection

DRTAs lend themselves well to some Web 2.0 tools, such as Google Docs or wikis. Students make predictions about what they expect to read in the text and post them in a Google Doc, sharing them with the group. Patterns emerge in the predictions. The most common predictions are not always accurate; the most creative may not be plausible. In the Google Doc or wiki, all the readers can read and comment on the predictions. As they read, they each provide evidence to revise or confirm any of the predictions, not just their own. Their own understanding evolves as it would in a face-to-face discussion but with the added benefit of time to reflect on and review the comments multiple times. After finishing the reading, the groups can decide on the key themes or ideas from the text based on their predictions and the proof collected from the text. After doing this on a common text as a group, readers can work on different texts with some commonality, such as texts by the same author, papers with conflicting viewpoints on the same topic, or texts from a single place or time. Their individual predictions, proof, and decisions provide the basis for drawing overall conclusions, having a discussion about common ideas, or developing a personal position on an issue.

Using the Technology—Google Docs

While it is almost without question that you have used Google to search for just about any-thing, and perhaps you have heard of Google Earth, you may or may not be using Google Docs. Google has developed a host of user applications, from documents to spreadsheets to blogs. Google Docs lets the users create documents, presentations, spreadsheets, forms, drawings, or tables that can then be shared with others electronically. One Google Doc can be shared with multiple users, and each person can help develop its content directly. To get started, you must first have a Google account. Once you have an account, you will need to add the Google Docs application. Then you are ready to create your first Google Doc.

Your new document should look familiar to you. In fact, it looks a lot like your word processing program on your own computer because it is modeled after it. So using it should be fairly intuitive. The benefits of using Google Docs are that you do not have to have a word processor, and it enables you to share a document with others and allows them to co-author the work with you. All the designated authors can write on the document just as if it were their own. Together, they can collaborate on this work, edit each other's additions, and publish. This same process works for spreadsheets, forms, drawings, and more. The new document is saved automatically on each author's Google Docs homepage where it can be downloaded, shared, edited, or deleted.

Google Docs offers some unique opportunities for student learning and collaboration in the classroom. One example has students developing writing portfolios. The Google space provides more than just a folder containing the student's work. It enables the teachers to monitor students' writing daily and keep track of changes. It also allows students to manage their work by sharing ideas, engaging in peer editing, making creative revisions, and publishing their work to a variety of digital platforms. Because Google Docs can be accessed while at school, at home, in the library, and with friends, writing becomes something that is part of all learning and not restricted to a particular classroom.

Wikis are another tool for multiple readers to write in a common space. A wiki website can be set up for free and has the similar advantages of a slide show for moving around and reorganiz-ing information, along with the benefits of web accessibility and group authorship.

CCSS Connection

- Interpret words and phrases as they are used in a text, including determining technical, connotative, and figurative meanings, and analyze how specific word choices shape meaning or tone.

Multiple authors can edit the wiki, building an understanding of a single text or a concept across texts. Viewing the history shows who has edited what, and authors can choose to be notified when a page is edited. Individual students can be "lead authors" of pages that answer a particular question, examine a prediction, or build an understanding of a concept. A teacher we worked with developed a wiki with his math class. He gave each of his students a page on the wiki where both the students and the teacher added problems and problem sets that they were working on. The students used their individual pages to work on problems and write about their thinking as they worked through them. Their teacher was then able to review their thinking, advise them on their work, direct them to see how other students were solving similar problems, and use the page as a record of their learning over time.

Reciprocal Teaching

In Reciprocal Teaching (Palinscar & Brown, 1984), students use four comprehension strategies—Questioning, Clarifying, Summarizing, and Predicting—to build on each other's thinking as they work through a text. As they read, they clarify any words or phrases that are unfamiliar or unclear, make predictions about what will come next for each section or chapter, and summarize the main ideas of what they have read. The teacher models how to lead discussions before and after reading using the strategies. The students can use the strategies independently for homework, writing down their questions, and making clarifications, summarizations, and predictions (Figure 1.4). The next day in class, students share their notes for each strategy in student-led groups. In the discussion groups, students share their thoughts and evidence from the text to support their predictions, and they add to their personal notes. These interactions are "reciprocal" in the sense that students respond to each other, making connections and building on each other's thinking.

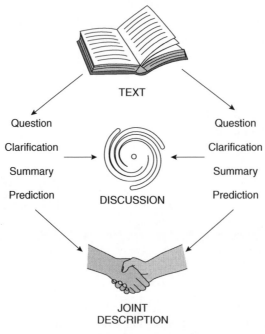

TEXT

Question	Question
Clarification	Clarification
Summary	Summary
Prediction	Prediction

DISCUSSION

JOINT
DESCRIPTION

Figure 1.4 Reciprocal teaching

Working in pairs, students can use technology in reciprocal teaching. First, each reader independently reads, recording her questions, needs for clarification, summaries of key ideas, and predictions for what will come next in the text. Then they compare documents and discuss each person's thinking. The purpose is to learn from each other's perspectives and ideas, so there is a lot of questioning and careful listening in the discussion. Together, the students summarize their new level of understanding based on their discussion, noting how their questions were answered, what clarifications were made, a summary of the section or chapter, and their predictions for the next section. Again here, VoiceThread presents itself as a tool to facilitate this type of activity.

Another version of Reciprocal Teaching is Internet Reciprocal Teaching, which is an adaption that builds on the same core principles. In Internet Reciprocal Teaching, the instructor first introduces students to the topic in an all-class setting, with each person constructing his or her own text while using the online reading strategies of questioning, locating, evaluating, synthesizing, and communicating. To engage students in Internet Reciprocal Teaching, first divide them into groups of four. Each student is assigned a role of either (1) summarizer, (2) questioner, (3) clarifier, or (4) predictor. Students then read a few paragraphs of the assigned text selection, taking notes on their computer as they go, and preparing for their role in the discussion. At a given point, the summarizer highlights the key ideas up to this point in the reading. The questioner then poses questions about the selection (puzzling information; connections; motivations of agents, actors, or characters; unclear parts). The clarifier then addresses confusing parts and attempts to answer them. The predictor then offers "educated guesses" about what the author will reveal next. Roles should rotate throughout the reading.

Double-Entry Journal

A double-entry journal (Figure 1.5) is another active reading strategy. If technology is not used, students fold a piece of paper in half vertically to crease it and then write key ideas from the text on the left side, and their reactions, questions, and connections on the right side. When using a

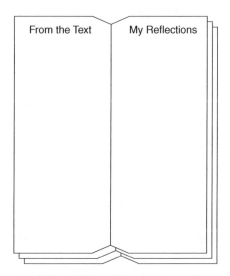

From the Text   My Reflections

Figure 1.5 Double-entry journal

word processor, students write the title of the text at the top, and then create a two-column by 10- to 12-row table. As they read, they can copy and paste key phrases or quotations into the left column, and react on the right. The digital advantage is that each box of the table expands with the ideas: Rows can be added, and text can be added at any time in the process anywhere in the document. If students are moving on to write about what they have read, they have valuable notes that they can cut and paste into a new document. The rows can be arranged as patterns emerge, such as time sequences or events that begin to make sense, or when a character has an important role in the plot. Columns can be added for page numbers if students are reading an expository text for specific quotes or for questions about notes taken. When doing research, tables from different sources can be integrated to provide a more complete picture. Try this with student writing. Have students exchange their essays or exploratory writing and do a double-entry journal as they read. Be sure they use the left column to "quote" the author and the right column to react to the work. This is especially effective for getting students an audience for their writing, since they can see how a reader reacts to their work.

Reviews and Annotations

Technology tools make it easier and more interesting for students to choose books. On the Internet, students can read published reviews and everyday reader reviews that are more than a book jacket read or a quick skim. With an advanced search at www.bookreview.com or www.goodreads.com, readers can search by author, publisher, or title or can choose only "must read" books. On either site, readers can also choose from listings of types of books, such as alternative health, art, bereavement, biographies, business, children's books, health and fitness, historical novels, horror, hard science, mystery, music, fiction (but not nonfiction), psychology, reference, romance, science fiction, travel, teen fiction and nonfiction, young adult fiction, and young adult nonfiction. The list of books under teen fiction includes a fantasy *Leven Thumps and the Whispered Secret* by Obert Skye, current events title *SQUAWK 7500* by Captain Steve A. Reeves, a historical novel *Kineo* by Christopher Keene, and the novel *Confessions of an Almost Movie Star* by Mary Kennedy.

Social Bookmarking

Goodreads.com is an example of social bookmarking. Social bookmarking is a means of organizing, storing, managing, and making searchable user information. There are many examples of social bookmarking websites, including Delicious (delicious.com), the site that popularized the terms "social bookmarking" and "tagging." Tagging offers users a way to organize their bookmarks so they can be shared with others. Bookmarked items are not owned but are refenced by the bookmarking system. Most often, bookmarks are publicly accessible, allowing others to view what has been marked and add what they like to their own bookmarks. Tags then allow bookmarks to be searched. Searching reveals what you have bookmarked and items you have tagged with similar tags. The real power is searching what others have tagged using the same tags as you have. Doing so may greatly expand the number of websites available to you that contain information about what you are looking for or studying. This occurs because you are building on the work of others in a community of learners exploring similar ideas. Here are nine ways to use bookmarking in your classroom:

1. Organize, filter, and store resources for the class on a local stewardship project.

2. Use a common group tag (hashtag) to share resources that students find in a candidate's viewpoint on foreign policy.

3. Reinforce lessons on primary and secondary sources by asking students to add sources to each collection with a justification for why it is a primary or secondary resource.

4. Promote discussions about what makes for high-quality sources by having students list their most reliable sources and then vote on each other's postings as being of high or low quality.

5. Create a school account for students to list their favorite readings with a recommendation for each one.

6. Have students review each other's collections and then talk about why they have chosen what they have.

7. Share tags with other faculty and classrooms and have fellow faculty become contributors.

8. Share a "Parent_resource" tag with the parent community that parents can subscribe to that covers what is being read in class and allows them to follow along at home.

9. Have students use smartphones to contribute while on the go.

At the *New York Times* book review page online (www.nytimes.com/pages/books/), students can read reviews of best-selling graphic books. Under children's book reviews, students will find reviews of paperback books for tween and teen readers with information on how many weeks they have been on the best-sellers list. The day I looked, *The Book Thief* by Markus Zusak had been on the list for 81 weeks! Now that is staying power! If you can provide the books for students or they can get them on their own, you can have them write their own reviews, have book discussion groups, or analyze why books that are popular meet the criteria for a best-selling book. Also under children's book reviews are the series books. As of April 1, 2009, Harry Potter had been on the list for 216 weeks.

The Book Spot (http://bookspot.com) offers lists of review sites, award-winning books, books by genre, where to buy books, where to find discussion guides, audio books, and "behind the book" information. This site has a children's section and a young adult section under each genre with booklists and short descriptions. One list is from the Carnegie Library of Pittsburgh where students can read reviews by other students and write their own. Sources for podcast reviews of books and interviews are also listed, including *Wordballoon: The Comic Book Interview Show* (wordballoon.blogspot.com); Just One More Book (http://justonemorebook.com) has podcast reviews for readers 4–10 years old that are great to listen to and are models for students to do their own audio reviews.

Other websites offer students search tools that allow them to identify their preferences and search for books by genre for reviews. For example, at http://allreaders.com, I chose the Sci-Fi/ Fantasy tab and then clicked on "Read a Book Review Online" at the top. This brought me to a page titled "Science Fiction Precision Booksearch *Powered By The Gordonator Precision Search Engine*" where I was prompted to click as few or as many options as I wished. For plot, I was able to choose the percentage of the book that is devoted to (1) chases or violence; (2) planning/ preparing, gathering information, debating puzzles/motives; (3) feelings, relationships, character bio/development; and (4) description of society, phenomena (tech), places. These are simple categories that students as readers or writers have as options. I was also able to choose the tone from a pull-down list, including very upbeat, depressing/sad, sensitive (sigh. . .), cynical or dry wit, humorous, suspenseful (sophisticated fear), or scary (primal ax-wielding fear). Now this list is particularly interesting for discussing tone and how it affects a story. I could also choose a mix of fantasy and science fiction. If this feels like too many decisions, there is a list of plots, which includes the following:

Animal story	Inner struggle	Romance
Clones	Life form altered	Spying and investigations
Coming of age	Mental/magical powers	Tech/$$$/info hunt
Cultural problems	Parody	Time travel
Explore/first contact	Political power play	Training/apprenticeship
Family relations	Religious overtones	War or invasion
Giant monster	Repressive society story	
Horror story	Robots, computers, VR	

I could choose these as the primary, secondary, and tertiary options, selecting all the themes I like and avoiding those I do not like. The last choice is age level: ages 7–14 or adult/young adult. I really wish this menu separated young adult from adult since young adult literature has emerged as a category in its own right, with main characters who are young adults. It helps that, in the next menu, there is a list of choices of the age of the main character: a kid, a teen, 20s–30s, 40s–50s, 60s–90s, and long-lived adults. There are more choices for the main adversary, setting, and style. My choices led to a list of books including *Dream Catcher* by Shauna Michaels, *The Protector* by Jenifer A. Ruth, *Altered Carbons* by Richard K. Morgan, *Tempting Danger* by Eileen Wilks, *F as in Frank* by David A. Page, and *Greenmantle* by Charles de Lint. Of the six books, I would probably read four of them, and I realized I need to find a way to eliminate werewolves in my next search—maybe "cynical" instead of "suspenseful" would do it.

This tool could be used to help students explore books they might want to read. Students could use the menus to decide what they like in a book they have just read and see if the site comes up with a list of recommended books. By reading the reviews of the top 10 books, they may become clearer about what they like, or perhaps they may redo their search to get books that they would be more likely to read. They can choose a book to read and share why they chose it, using the language of the menus. Explicitly, this site gets them to identify what they like, read reviews, and choose a book to read. Implicitly, they learn about options for plot, characters, setting, and style that will help them understand what they read and give them options for new kinds of reading. It could also be used to help them identify elements for a story they wish to write.

CCSS Connection

- Integrate and evaluate content presented in diverse formats and media, including visually and quantitatively, as well as in words.

The Back Story

Another opportunity for using technology to enrich reading fiction or nonfiction texts is to use the Internet to find the back story and context for a text. Biographies, information on context, history, and commentary are all available. Students are used to seeing the "making of the movie" and outtakes or commentary on movies so they understand the concept. Reading "around" a story or text brings a depth and breadth to understanding not possible from reading in isolation. It also leads to more reading and thinking since students locate other texts that are interesting to them. Sometimes knowing when and where something happened or what an author was experiencing in her life while she was writing something can make it more interesting to students since it grounds it in life experience.

Challenge students to find at least two other sources for any idea in the textbook, curriculum, or the novel they are reading and incorporate it into the class discussion or an individual essay. The goal here is not necessarily to find sources that agree or disagree. You could have students find one of each, two of one type or the other, or two that relate to an area of the text that is under discussion or has presented itself as a challenge for the class. As noted earlier, at Book Spot (http://bookspot.com) readers can find out about authors, publishers, literary critics, podcasts, book associations, book events, book facts, book news, literary magazines, and literacy. Brief descriptions of the lives and work of some authors are featured with links to their homepages.

Living authors probably have their own official website. For example, Eric Carle and Jan Brett, both famous award-winning children's authors, have interactive websites inviting readers to explore and learn more about the author and their books.

If an author is deceased, devotees of their work may have created a website, such as the Jane Austen website (www.pemberley.com/janeinfo/janeinfo.html), which has discussion boards for each of her novels. For example, there are discussions of what Mr. Darcy expected of his future wife, whether "rencontre" signals an unpleasant meeting or simply an unexpected one, and the evolution of Charlotte's attitudes. For each of these topics and more there are multiple responses by several different people. Students could be assigned to read through the discussion, respond to some questions, post their own questions, and report about the experience. Were the questions provocative, interesting, nitpicking, or text-based? What was the tone of the responses? Who participates in these discussions? Why? If one of our goals is to both empower and interest students in lifelong reading, then this kind of website discussion is something they may wish to participate in.

Other online book groups have discussion areas for current works that begin with a review and questions and invite other readers to make comments. *The Times*, a United Kingdom newspaper's online edition, uses this format and even gives away copies of some of the books (see http://entertainment.timesonline.co.uk/tol/arts_and_entertainment/books/books_group). Reviewing these kinds of sites, and especially contributing to them, helps students see discussing books as an adult activity that is sought out by interesting people, rather than merely as a school assignment.

Face-to-face book groups are also supported on the Internet. Reader's Circle (www.readerscircle.org/) offers a database of book clubs—where members read the same book—and reader's groups, where they come to talk about whatever they are reading. The site lists over 800 clubs and 189 authors available for over-the-phone visits with groups that are reading their books.

CCSS Connection

- Delineate and evaluate the argument and specific claims in a text, including the validity of the reasoning as well as the relevance and sufficiency of the evidence.
- Assess how point of view or purpose shapes the content and style of a text.

Consider modeling some class discussions after book groups to teach students to interact constructively. Sometimes called "literature circles," students meet in groups of four to six to discuss, respond to, and reflect on their reading of a common book (see literaturecircles.com for more info). Teach students how to take different roles in the groups and to build on each other's ideas. You can make up the roles based on the skills and strategies you want students to focus on, or use these: a facilitator or discussion director, connector (makes connections from text to self, to life, or to other texts), reporter (summarizes key ideas for each session), wordsmith (collects interesting words or phrases), and a style minder (notes interesting ways the author writes).

If I understood what Helena just said, I think _____.
I want to go back to what Jaime said about _____. It made me think.
If I put what Jorge said about _____ with what Latisha said about _____, I come up with _____.

This passage reminds me of what you said about _____.
I'm not sure I understand what you said, can you say more?

Book blogs are also something to explore with students. They can find them on a list on a website such as Book Group Buzz (http://bookgroupbuzz.booklistonline.com) or create their own. A lot of book blogs are like a reader's diary, where the bloggers reflect on what they are reading, explore other titles, and discuss literary issues and themes.

For example, one called, "A Work in Progress: Adventures in (mostly) reading, and (sometimes) needlework and other artsy endeavors" explores "middlebrow" literature, written mostly by women for women from the 1920s to 1950s (http://danitorres.typepad.com/workinprogress). This literature was evidently considered too "easy, insular and smug" but was enormously popular. The blogger quotes a book about these novels, *The Feminine Middlebrow Novel: 1920s to 1950*, and lists some novels in that category including *The Bread Giver* by Anzia Yerzierska and *So Big* by Edna Ferber. A great assignment would be to have students create their own reader blogs, beginning with putting a novel they are reading in the context of its genre, type, and/or period.

Words

Online access to dictionaries and word sites can provide quick support for students while reading and perhaps pique their interest in words in general. Merriam-Webster has a free online dictionary. Onelook.com lets you type in parts of words if you do not know how to spell the whole word and then produces definitions from multiple online dictionaries. A search on the word "scruple" yielded definitions from 37 dictionaries, including that it refers to an apothecary's weight of 20 grains, as well as the fear that something is a sin when it is not. At www.wordcentral.com, students can search new words and add their own and use the standard dictionary or thesaurus. There's a daily "buzz word" complete with usage and word origins.

You can have students collect words they particularly like from their reading or are having trouble with. Traditionally, words would be written on note cards or into a notebook. A few more modern ways, allowing students to access their "notecards" both in the classroom or while at home are to (1) have a file on their laptop, if you are in a one-to-one school; (2) keep a Google Doc as a running library; or (3) have them create a word cloud with their favorite words used in a story. Although this is a favorite strategy to use with younger children to develop their vocabulary, many authors also collect words for their beauty, sound, or power that they later incorporate into their work. J.R.R. Tolkien wrote about the phrase "cellar door" as having an especially beautiful sound: "The nature of this pleasure is difficult, perhaps impossible, to analyze. It cannot, of course, be discovered by structural analysis. No analysis will make one either like or dislike a language, even if it makes more precise some of the features of style that are pleasing or distasteful" (1955, p. 22). If students collect the words they like in Excel, they can sort them alphabetically. If they add where they got the word, the definition, and why they like it, they will have thought about the word, are likely to use it in conversation or in their writing, and certainly recognize it in their reading.

Many applications also have built-in dictionaries. For example, the Macintosh operating system lets you select a word, Control-click it, and choose "Look up in Dictionary." Working in Microsoft Word or Google Docs, you can also highlight a word and get its definition.

Nonfiction Reading

Nonfiction reading, or reading in the content areas, benefits from strategies we have already discussed such as SQ3R and DRTA. While some purists claim that SQ3R is only for expository texts, and DRTA and book groups are only for narrative text, many teachers have successfully used each of the strategies with all kinds of texts. At their core, they share the conscious use of strategies to think about the text before, during, and after reading and to process the main ideas in writing.

CCSS Connection

- Analyze how two or more texts address similar themes or topics in order to build knowledge or to compare the approaches the authors take.
- Read and comprehend complex literary and informational texts independently and proficiently.

Reading content on the web involves some additional skills and strategies. Students need to identify the authors of the information and their credentials, consider the extent to which they address a topic, and consult multiple sources. All this can make reading the nonfiction material more interesting, as the reader tries to verify the accuracy the text. This is a form of media literacy and has come front and center into classrooms. We address this very important issue more in the coming chapters.

For example, have students read to figure out whether they can do anything about global climate change. To illustrate this, let us investigate climate change and, along the way, make our thinking apparent by writing notes as we explore the authors, their credentials, evidence provided, and its accuracy (see Figure 1.6). This is a modeling exercise that can often help students new to Internet exploration learn to carefully and critically read information. We take notes on our exploration in a simplified format using a word processing program on a personal computer. This is also a very effective exercise when done using a collaborative space (wiki or Google Doc) and students are reading and taking notes in small groups. An exhaustive search might take many class periods and additional time at home to sort through the information gathered. The *first part* entitled "We begin" is an outline of the searches and the results. It shows the search keywords, results, which result was chosen, and what information was available from that link. The *second part* is the detailed notes from the document open during the search. The document contains the data collected, links for sourcing the material, questions (marked with asterisks), and any additional information important to the search. *Finally*, we are able to come to a reasonable conclusion based on our research and critical reading of all available material. See the example in Figure 1.6.

Projected Sea-Level Rise in the Maldives

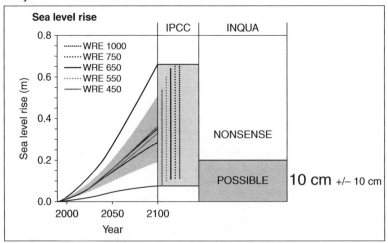

Source: Nils-Axel Mörner.
Dr. Mörner was president of the International Union for Quaternary Research's (INQUA) Commission on Sea-Level Changes and Coastal Evolution (1999–2003). Its research proved that the catastrophic predictions of the Intergovernmental Panel on Climate Change (IPCC), based on computer models of the effects of global warming, are "nonsense."

Figure 1.6 Example using global climate change

Summary

Technology tools support reading in interesting and provocative ways. They pose challenges as well. The sheer amount of information available means that students need to learn to read and process information differently than they do with print. Using technology tools with strategies such as SQ3R and DRTA gives students valuable experience in using the technology for tracking their own understanding and organizing their thoughts as they read. These skills need to then be explicitly transferred to processing hypertext and the vast amount of information available on the Internet.

2 Technology Tools for Writing

Forget all the rules. Forget about being published. Write for yourself and celebrate writing.

—Melinda Haynes

Fill the paper with the breathings of your heart.

—William Wordsworth

Technology has contributed to writing by making it more flexible and more authentic through providing access to more audiences, and more access to writers and their work. These are qualities we have used for years to get students to want to write. Frank Smith (1998) pointed out many years ago that the only time it is worthwhile to correct students' writing is when they ask you to; his statement is at once radical and commonsensical. Only when students care enough to attend to feedback will they benefit from it. Publishing, even for one's self, is one way to increase how much students care about the quality of their writing. The computer and the Internet have made self-publishing the norm, and access to ideas, people, and places commonplace. The individual voice is seen as a worthy perspective and can be followed by thousands of people or kept private as a kind of diary. In this chapter we explore ways to use technology to teach students how to write and how to think about writing in their lives.

Digital Writing Tools

As we explored in the chapter on reading, there are many different digital tools for taking notes and reflecting. Word processors support text with graphics and links in a mostly linear format. HyperCard-type tools such as Keynote and PowerPoint support a "stack of individual pages" that have text, graphics, and links. Web pages support hypertext in the online environment and may be private or public. Although these formats have different purposes, they are somewhat interchangeable. Word documents can be saved as .html (hypertext markup language) for the web. PowerPoint presentations can also be saved as webpages or pictures. Webpages can be saved as "print friendly" or text copied and pasted into word documents. You will probably want to discuss each of these formats with students so they become conversant in how to choose a tool for expression and know how to make each one work for them. We discuss how and when each tool can be used in the sections on prewriting, drafting, and publishing.

As Newman wrote way back in 1984, writing digitally has huge advantages over paper. The writer can almost see her thoughts becoming text, experimenting with words that sound right or look right according to what she has in her head. The intention and its expression hang in suspended animation, side by side, at once better connected and yet explicitly separate. The contribution to "flow" seems to come from a combination of how easy it is to produce text that is satisfying and, at the same time, how easy it is to edit in large and small ways. We have always urged students to start their writing with something they were thinking or experiencing and then build on it, but that was difficult to do on paper. Note cards were more flexible, but copying over or rewriting interrupted the flow of thinking and took a lot of time—time that didn't seem to contribute to the thinking. All this flexibility with digital text means young writers really can think and act like the much more motivated published authors, who seem not to have minded the tedium of production all these years, or at least persevered through it. Young writers can now have "works in progress" that they think about and revise, send to others for feedback, and create over a period of time.

Publishing also has radically changed. For the average person, the lag time between being able to read in a medium and being able to write in that medium is shrinking. Almost 5,000 years went by from the invention of writing before Gutenberg's 1440 printing press made texts more available and created more authors. It was another 500 years before books were widely available for purchase and in public libraries. However, writing still was exclusive to a few people who had to rely on publishers for printing and distribution. Finally, the Internet has made self-publishing easy with the potential of a large audience finding the work through search engines.

The forms of "writing" have also changed. Now video, audio, and graphics are all available for expression alone or together with text. In contrast with the written word, it took only about 100 years from the invention of video for the tools to become commonly available for many people to produce their own. Now journalists, authors, thinkers, and students can use all these forms of expression in many different ways. Blogs, wikis, unsponsored websites, online books, reviews of books and products, and many more forms of expression exist on the Internet.

The number and type of audiences for student writers have also changed. Instead of writing for the teacher or to get a grade, students can publish their work on the web and get feedback from others. They can maintain their own websites in the form of blogs, wikis, or pages of their own designs. They can self-publish and measure their success through the webpage hits their work generates. They can write for online publications, comment on others' writing, and join discussion groups. All these tools are becoming the natural forms of expression that they turn to for information in their lives outside of school. They need to be taught about and encouraged to use these forms of expression *in* school.

CCSS Connection

- Develop and strengthen writing as needed by planning, revising, editing, rewriting, or trying a new approach. Use technology, including the Internet, to produce and publish writing and to interact and collaborate with others.

Figure 2.1 Languages and numbers of articles on Wikipedia

One example of a large information source is Wikipedia (Figure 2.1) with its nearly 8.5 million articles in 250+ languages, as of early 2011. Wikipedia is an example of "crowdsourcing," in which the public is invited to contribute to a task or solve a problem (Carvin, 2009). For this kind of resource, the contribution of individuals creates a resource for many people often at a fraction of the cost of traditionally assembling the resources, or in situations where creating it would be impossible without the contributions of a large number of people. "Apps for Democracy" was a competition to create applications of publicly available data about Washington, DC, that resulted in websites for historical tours, locating services, and finding parking. "The Hurricane Information Center" was created as a Ning for people to share information about Hurricane Gustav in 2008. Whatever digital venue students choose to frequent, they can probably also contribute, so writing opportunities abound.

Using the Technology—Wordle

It is likely that you have seen a Wordle or even created your own. What we like so much about them is how clear they can make the meaning of a piece of writing for a child. To get started, go to Wordle.net. Then, click "Create Your Own." Copy and paste in a passage or have the students use a piece of their own writing and hit "Go." The images produced are yours to use as you wish. Figure 2.2 shows what the creation page for a Wordle looks like.

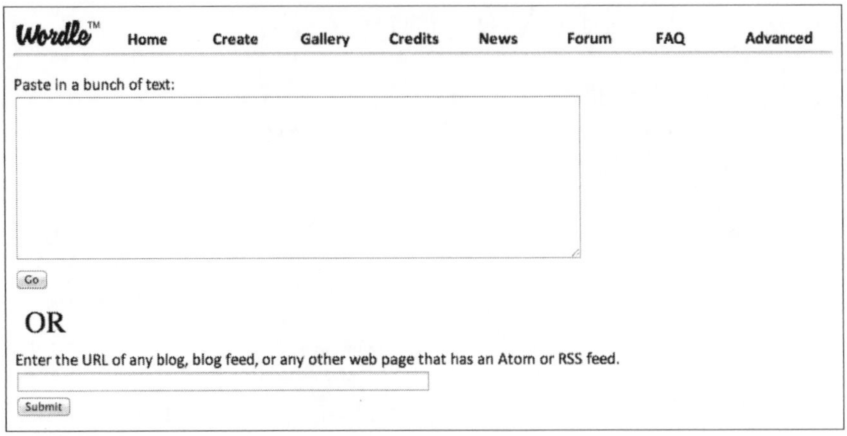

Figure 2.2 Wordle creation page

A Wordle may be a great way to introduce a text, analyze a piece of writing for content and themes, illustrate to students their use of language, and do numerous other creative tasks. You may also choose to look at the many Wordles that have been created.

Technology Support for Prewriting

Prewriting involves activities to explore ideas, brainstorm what to include, talk through ideas or do background research, create an outline or map to work from, or otherwise become clear about what will be written. Students need help identifying ideas that they are sufficiently interested in to actually pursue throughout the writing process. While students need support throughout the writing process to sustain their confidence, get feedback, and develop their skills, helping them get an idea and planning together in the prewriting stage get them off to a very good start.

Where do writing ideas come from? Many students spend time surfing the net and shopping and networking online. Pew's Generations Online in 2009 interview results show 93% of 12–17-year-olds use the Internet, the highest of any age group. Sixty-three percent (63%) of teens use the Internet to get news and 78% play games online (Jones & Fox, 2009). Students can be prompted and taught how to use the Internet to explore topics of interest and find models for writing to get them excited about expressing themselves in writing.

Students are already writing. All teens report they write in schools, and 93% say they write for their own pleasure. Parents believe teens write more today than they did when they were that age (Lenhart, Arafeh, Smith, & Macgill, 2008). Teens report they are motivated to write for school when they:

1. Can choose topics related to their interests and lives
2. Have the opportunity to write creatively
3. Have adults who challenge them with interesting curricula
4. Have adults who give them detailed feedback
5. Write for an audience

CCSS Connection

Write routinely over extended time frames (time for research, reflection, and revision) and shorter time frames (a single sitting or a day or two) for a range of tasks, purposes, and audiences.

Building on Interests with Blogs

To build on this motivation, assign students to find out more about a topic of interest to them and create a blog as they find out more information. Have them link their blog to their social networking profile and find at least three other blogs by people interested in the same topic. Have them report every day to a few other students in the class about what is new on their blog. Set up preview days in which the blog author shows the site to other students. Make part of the assignment visiting each other's blogs and commenting, adding resources and ideas, asking questions, and offering encouragement. Students might choose anime, Formula One racing, a music group they like, a destination to visit, a societal problem (drug use), or anything else as the topic of their blog. Free blogs can be set up at blogspot.com, blogger.com, livejournal.com, wordpress.com, and other sites that can be reached by searching for "free blog."

There are a ton of project ideas out there for using blogs in the classroom. One of the best articles we have read on the subject listed 45+ ideas. We have chosen three of our favorite ideas and listed them here. If you are still stuck after reading ours, a quick Google search will find you many more.

1. For the teacher, we like using the blog as a place to post homework assignments and notes for students and parents. If you are able to post a few days of assignments or a long-term project description, it gives students a way to plan ahead and check their progress and parents a way to connect with what their child is working on.

2. Student vacation/trip/travel blogs are a great way to keep students engaged with learning while away from school. We recognize that one of the most powerful ways students learn is through experience, so why not make the connection to learning. Students enjoy posting photos of their trips and time away from school, and others enjoy reading about what their friends are doing. Teacher blogs of travel have been used very successfully to help students gain an understanding of different cultures and languages.

3. Poetry writing blogs are a great way to engage students throughout the day both in and out of school. Giving an assignment to write a poem and to post it to their blog (or class blog) allows students to read other's work and be inspired to write wherever they are, not just while in class. This is also a great tool for those using flipped classrooms.

Start with Data

Another inquiry activity is to start with data. Either give students data or have them find data on a topic of interest to them. In this activity, which was identified as an effective practice in the 2007 Carnegie meta-analysis, students focus on making sense of the data and communicating it to others (Graham & Perin, 2007b). For example, NASA has live data feeds that would be good to use for this activity. At the Space Weather Action Center, http://sunearthday.nasa.gov/swac/data.php, students will find tutorials and live data for tracking sunspots, identifying storm signals, and studying the magnetosphere and auroras. All-sky cameras capture the images shown on the site. Students interpret the images and draw conclusions about auroras from these satellite images and ground-based observatories in Alaska. If students are interested in any of these topics, they can first ask questions they would like to have answered from or about the data, identify an audience for what they find out, and write about both the content and the process of their research into the data. Working with data often extends into multiple disciplines and so is a great way to team with other teachers (math and science) to develop collaborative learning projects for individual students or your entire class.

Models Spark Ideas

Sometimes a model can prompt an idea for writing. Students will see a website that models an approach or format to a topic and be inspired to create something similar. Student-created websites may be particularly inspiring to other students. Student work can be viewed at http://thewritesource.com/studentmodels for grades 6–8 and 9–12 from Houghton Mifflin (Figure 2.3). Each model has a short overview, such as this one for *The Racist Warehouse:*

> *This personal narrative by eighth-grader Alicia presents an engaging voice. Read the essay and notice how Alicia's personality comes through; she obviously cares about her subject. Her use of details gives the reader a clear picture of the characters and environment in this account of Alicia's first encounter with racism.* (http://thewritesource.com/studentmodels/ws2k-racism.htm)

One interactive writer's model site is at http://go.hrw.com/eolang/modbank. Students can click on the notes in the margin to learn more about the piece of writing from the labels and highlighted text. For example, the notes on the left for "Writing an Autobiography," for the piece

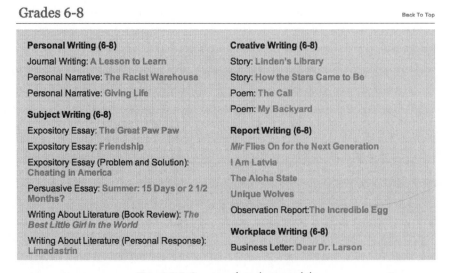

Figure 2.3 Source of student models

My Mother's Shoes, begin with an introduction, engaging opening, and background information. Choosing "Engaging Opening" causes that text to turn blue in color, as well as the text in the autobiography that is an engaging opening. Students can not only read the piece for inspiration but they can also revisit it after they start writing to better understand the elements of the form.

CCSS Connection

- Produce clear and coherent writing in which the development, organization, and style are appropriate to task, purpose, and audience.

The Greece Central School District has its own set of models with detailed critiques embedded in the files. For example, the "Literary Response" model paper from an 11th grader received high praise for its opening paragraph: "The writer chose the perfect sentence patterns to express the paradox of post WWII America; contrasting pairs in the first and third sentences emphasize the paradox" (annotations, p. 1) (see www.greece.k12.ny.us/instruction/ELA/6-12/Writing/Exem plars/Grade%2011%20Literary%20Response.pdf). This kind of specificity goes beyond telling students what to do to showing them how to do it.

Brainstorming

Brainstorming is almost certainly something you yourself have employed when working with others and have likely used with your students. Brainstorming is a way to explore what is known about an idea or of finding a creative solution to a problem. It is an excellent strategy to use with inclusion classrooms and to tap into prior student knowledge, be inclusive, remove fear from learning, try something new, and tap into inherent student creativity and imagination.

There is no specific size to the brainstorming group, but most suggest a size somewhere between 8 and 12 participants. When done face to face, a brainstorming session requires a facilitator, a good space to work in, and things to write with and on. The facilitator's job is to capture what is being said (the ideas), guide the session, and encourage all to participate. These jobs can be given to three different group members as well—leader, scribe, and team member. There are four basic rules when conducting a brainstorming session: (1) no criticism, (2) welcoming the unusual, (3) quantity wanted, and (4) combining and improving on ideas. The brainstorming process starts with a problem statement that needs to be specific enough to help the participants focus on a solution while being open-ended enough to allow for creative thinking. Brainstorming adapts well to virtual learning spaces and tools as well. There are no technology tools that are designed specifically for brainstorming. Rather, there are many tools that make visible the student thinking and idea generation that are at the heart of the brainstorming process.

While brainstorming sessions are typically conducted face to face, one of our favorites occurred online. The teacher had the students working on a problem-based learning scenario about the death of Meriwether Lewis of the Lewis and Clark team of explorers. How did he die? What clues from his life and work and that final trip do students want to uncover? As a homework assignment, students were given a link to a shared Google Doc and asked to brainstorm ideas, directions, images, challenges, and solutions for the investigation that evening. The next day, the teacher had the students create new Google docs for the key investigation areas to be explored in the second phase of the project.

Email, Text Messaging, Blogging, and Online Discussion Spaces for Ideas

Teens are writing all the time in digital environments. Eighty-five percent (85%) say they engage in some form of personal electronic communication some of the time, but 60% do not see this as "writing" (Lenhart et al., 2008). Some people have suggested that rather than contributing to the development of student writing, these short informal digital messages affect student writing negatively (Dillon, 2008). However, most students do not believe their informal communication has a negative effect on their writing development. We would suggest that this ongoing rapid communication can be harnessed to fuel the development of student interest in writing, give them ideas for writing, and help them develop opinions or become aware of issues they may wish to write about in more depth. These tools are increasingly being used for social activism, reporting on fast-breaking events, emergency notifications, and political activism. To get started, use a simple tool like PollsAnywhere.com to have students text their predictions for the weather to introduce a unit on climate versus weather. Take the pulse of their understanding with additional polls and show them the results. Have them write about how their understanding has changed.

CCSS Connection

- Write routinely over extended time frames (time for research, reflection, and revision) and shorter time frames (a single sitting or a day or two) for a range of tasks, purposes, and audiences.
- Use technology, including the Internet, to produce and publish writing and to interact and collaborate with others.

Jottings

Ask students to think about how they currently use text messages or other communication media and to incorporate that into a short story or essay. Brainstorm with them about what they can observe about these kinds of communication. Do people communicate differently under different conditions? Is it possible to have a writing style in these media? What are the main topics of communication? Are there peak times for communicating? This will get students observing their communication, becoming more conscious of what and how they are communicating, and get them thinking about it as a source of ideas.

As students show interest in ideas, have them keep a log with "jottings" (Topping & McManus, 2002). These jottings are information, sources, ideas, and connections and become a collection they can draw from to create a draft. If you are using writing to learn content, these jottings will be about the topic under study. You can also have students text their "jottings" to a blog, creating a running list of them. Periodically, they can mine the blog for writing ideas or reflect on any patterns they see in their postings.

RAFT—Choices Writers Make

To emphasize that this writing is not just for the teacher for a grade, suggest students use the **RAFT** strategy:

Role—What is your role as a writer? What perspective will you present?
Audience—Who will read what you write? Why do you want THEM to read it?
Format—What format will be best to make your point? Letter, article, poem, story?
Topic—What is the focus of your writing?

We know that having choices around their writing is motivating to students. Using RAFT, you can give student writers choices about their role, the audience, and the format, even if you give them the topic. Having those choices makes them more aware of their choices as an author and can create more of a sense of responsibility for making those choices. Having made their own choices, students also feel more of a sense of pride in the successful completion of writing based on those choices.

CCSS Connection

- Produce clear and coherent writing in which the development, organization, and style are appropriate to task, purpose, and audience.

To use RAFT with technology support, make it a template in their writing folder. For each piece they write, models they like, or other students' work, have them identify the RAFT. This collection becomes a personal reference and a constant reminder that writing always involves making decisions about the **R**ole, **A**udience, **F**ormat, and **T**opic.

The use of technology to support prewriting may be more a shift of perspective about where ideas come from for teachers and students and how to parlay students' communication efforts into a source of ideas. Having students use their lives as the basis for their writing is not new. It may just be that their pervasive use of technology makes it a new, unexamined source and fertile ground for ideas. For example, take an event in the history curriculum like the Boston Tea Party and create a menu of options for Role, Audience, and Format. Students might take the role of a patriot, a British sympathizer, a bystander, a Canadian, or a Frenchman. Make a list of all the roles students can think of. Do the same for Audience. Are they writing for someone like themselves, someone on the same side, or someone on the opposite side? What formats could they use? Their brainstorm might include posters, pamphlets, newspaper articles, speeches, or letters. Once you have all the lists, students can choose a Role, an

Audience, and a Format to use in their writing. Doing all this electronically in a shared folder, Google Doc, or wiki lets students see each other's' work and ideas as they develop and can push them to create something unique.

Drafting and Revising Using Technology

As the research shows and we discussed in the chapter on reading, digital tools make writing easier—from getting ideas out to shaping a narrative or essay, to rearranging whole sections, crafting sentences, and editing for spelling and grammar. Digital tools provide opportunities to write longer, to write better, and for the process to focus on creativity rather than the mechanics of production. Freed from the mechanics of writing, students can move from "knowledge-telling" to "knowledge-transformation" in which the writer uses the process of writing to extend ideas, reason through something, and increase personal awareness of a situation or idea (Bereiter & Scardamalia, 1987, pp. 5–6).

CCSS Connection

- Develop and strengthen writing as needed by planning, revising, editing, rewriting, or trying a new approach.

Each technology tool for writing has underlying assumptions in its design that determine the features that are predominant and easy to use. It is important to engage students in discussions of these assumptions so they can choose and use the tools that best serve their writing purpose. In this section, we discuss word processors, presentation tools, and websites. We recommend introducing one tool at a time with examples and then letting students choose from among the tools they have learned in class or on their own.

Word Processors for Writing

Word processors are good for longer linear pieces such as essays, articles, chapters, narratives, and poetry. They also support publishing pamphlets, flyers, or bulletins based on built-in templates. They support interesting formatting for any text with a large variety of fonts, colors, styles, text boxes, and inserted pictures or graphics. For research papers, the footnote and citation function smooths out the process of attribution to sources. Links can be embedded for sources or websites on the Internet. Word processing can be done traditionally on a single computer, freely with Zoho (writer.zoho.com), or collectively on Google (google.docs.com). Being an efficient user of a computer's word processor takes practice. Having students become regular users of such a technology tool will go a long way toward their continued success in all subject areas and beyond. We like to encourage students to experiment with the word processing features. For example, in the first draft of an essay on J. K. Rowling's effect on young people's interest in reading, have them use word art on the title. In the second draft, have them add graphics, pictures, or maps and refer to them in the text. In the third draft, have them add links and references in footnotes. By staging the additions, students use the tools to construct new levels of meaning in their writing.

Presentation Tools for Writing

Presentation tools are good for slide shows, taking notes on individual slides so they can be rearranged later, presenting an overview, or documenting a process. Internal linking can be used to create a table of contents and then jump to the slides that support each section.

Font sizes and styles, bullet formatting, and text boxes support a lot of flexibility for presenting text, graphics, and images. These "objects" can then be choreographed to appear with different effects automatically or with a click. Effects can be used to convey meaning, with options of objects appearing or fading; zooming in from the left, right, above, or below; disintegrating; or exploding. Music, audio, and video fields can be added to contribute to the meaning.

CCS Connection

- Produce clear and coherent writing in which the development, organization, and style are appropriate to task, purpose, and audience.
- Use technology, including the Internet, to produce and publish writing and to interact and collaborate with others.

Presentation tools such as these are just that—tools. They are only as good as the information presented with/on/in them. Some of the tools are more user friendly and easier to get started with. If you are already familiar with Google Docs or other Google tools, Google Presenter is likely for you. If you are looking to "up" your presentation game or challenge your students to truly make something original, have a look at Prezi.

Here are some ideas for using digital presentation tools in student writing:

- Help students create digital stories, e-scrapbooks, projects, and reports.
- Teach students about creating effective presentations.
- Provide a way for students to collaborate and work collectively.
- Provide multimedia alternatives for book reports.
- Enhance student visual engagement.
- Provide accessibility for challenged students.
- Use as a template for beginning students.
- Include multimedia and images to tell a story.

By the way, don't worry if students start playing around with the formatting, colors, and special effects *before* the content is complete. We have noticed that there are several benefits to this for many students. It often helps to keep them interested, helps them to think about how the ideas are fitting together, and makes them think about their audience and how to engage them.

Websites for Writing

Web-based pages are good for reaching an Internet audience and making writing accessible anytime from anywhere. From constructed pages coded using hypertext markup language (html) to premade templates or tools such as wikis and blogs, Internet pages have all the features of word processing and presentation tools. They can have multiple fonts, colors, styles, and features with music, video, audio, and graphics, including special effects motion files. Hypertext lends itself to providing samples or beginnings of longer texts with the invitation to read "more . . ."

Websites for Writing

- Google pages—http:// pages.google.com
- pageflakes—www.pageflakes.com
- protopage—www.protopage.com

Websites require thoughtfulness about how the media affect the message—how media "massage" what people understand and where they focus their attention. In 1952 Marshall McLuhan wrote about the "retribalization" that media would bring—the feeling of connectedness brought about by meaning conveyed through multiple media.

The design of the website is more immersive than a word-processed document or a presentation. The writer is able to use it as a table of contents, a sampler for longer pieces, for attention-getting features that point to what is new, or an archive of a collection of writing pieces. Blogs and wikis have a culture of the author reflecting on his or her current ideas or events in society and archiving them over time. Discussion spaces are more immediate, capturing the give and take of conversation or of people responding to others' ideas.

In the past, instruction in writing has engaged students in thinking about their options for type, genre, style, and organization. Now it needs to include understanding media well enough to make conscious choices about how to express themselves. Fortunately, students are immersed in these media, so they bring that experience to the task. What they lack is the insight to make it work for them.

Designing a webpage is a great way to help students express themselves. A personal webpage is something that can be continued throughout their school experience and expanded and adapted as needed. Student websites can become a great way to manage school work and develop student learning portfolios if your school does not offer them. The format of a webpage is something that students are very familiar with and are often very interested in developing. We have seen many examples of student websites and are continually impressed by their work, skill, and passion. To get started, ask your students to find three to five websites of individuals—either students, professionals, or hobbyists—that they really like. Have them use these websites to come up with criteria for what makes a good website, especially one they would create for themselves.

Teaching Writing Strategies with Wikis, Presentation Tools, and Webpages

Instruction in strategies for drafting, revising, and editing their compositions has a positive effect on student writing (Graham & Perin, 2007b). Effective instruction includes modeling, explaining how to use a strategy, and giving students feedback on their use of the strategies.

CCS Connection

- Develop and strengthen writing as needed by planning, revising, editing, rewriting, or trying a new approach.
- Use technology, including the Internet, to produce and publish writing and to interact and collaborate with others.

Self-Regulated Strategy Development (SRSD) is an approach to help students learn specific strategies for planning, drafting, and revising text. Students are treated as active collaborators in the learning process. Instruction by the teacher is in six stages (De La Paz & Graham, 2002; Harris & Graham, 1996):

1. Develop background knowledge about the strategy.
2. Describe the strategy—its purpose and benefits.
3. Model how to use the strategy.
4. Memorize the steps of the strategy and any accompanying mnemonic.
5. Provide support from the teacher to support or scaffold student mastery of the strategy.
6. Enable independent use by students with few or no supports.

Wikis

pbworks—http://pbworks.com
wikispaces—www.wikispaces.com
jottit—http://jottit.com
mediawiki—www.mediawiki.org
zoho wiki—http://wiki.zoho.com
wetpaint—www.wetpaint.com
writeboard—www.writeboard.com

Technology can help you introduce each strategy through examples and templates and then lets you store these aids in a common space for students to use and refer to as they do their own writing. Consider creating a wiki or other tool to post the strategies you teach with examples so students have constant access to them. You can ask students to reflect on how they used the strategy as part of the writing process, annotating the text as they work through it. Their reflections can be housed with their writing to provide a picture of their writing process, allowing you to discover areas where they need further coaching or instruction.

Consciously using strategies helps students develop self-regulation skills like knowing when a strategy works, how to be sure to use it well, and knowing how successful they are in using it.

Remembering Writing Strategies

A common technique for helping students remember a strategy is a mnemonic device such as a word where each letter stands for a step in the process. Three drafting/revising strategies are **PLAN, WRITE** (De La Paz & Graham, 2002; Harris & Graham, 1996), and **ARMS** (Topping & McManus, 2002).

PLAN—*a strategy for responding to a prompt (planning matters)*
P*ay attention to the prompt*
L*ist the main idea*
A*dd supporting ideas*
N*umber your ideas*

WRITE—*a strategy for a thesis paper (just "write" it)*
W*ork from your plan to develop your thesis statement*
R*emember your goals*
I*nclude transition words for each paragraph*
T*ry to use different kinds of sentences*
E*xciting, interesting, $10,000 words*

ARMS—*a strategy for revising a text (get your "arms" around it)*
A*dd text to elaborate, complement, or extend what you want to say*
R*emove text that is unnecessary or confusing*
M*ove text to create a clearer organization*
S*ubstitute text to better say something*

Use technology to have students create podcasts about each strategy. They can do raps, rhymes, or songs. Post all these online for downloading so they can listen to them on their music players. Create a wiki called "writing strategies" and post each one. Invite students to add their personal versions, comment on the strategies as they use (and abuse) them, and add examples and reviews about how they work.

Using a Rubric with Technology Support

A rubric describes different levels of quality for the key elements. Meant to be a qualitative tool, the levels are nevertheless numbered so the paper can be "scored." We prefer to use rubrics that are descriptive of each level of quality, such as a first draft where the writer could say, "I write about some things I have heard about the topic," to what a writer might say at the fluid level: "I make my point by choosing the most interesting and important ideas to tell the reader in an interesting, fun way." The idea is that each rating is a developmental level. It captures how different writers think and go about writing. At any level, the writer can look to the next higher level to improve, which is more reachable and understandable than two levels higher. This Vygotskian idea of a zone of development supports gradual improvement. The challenge is to identify the levels that people normally go through in getting better. Table 2.1 is a rubric for the writer to think about his or her work and revise it. The writer reads the question at the top aloud and then each of the statements to see which one best fits the quality of the writing at this stage.

Writer's Rubric—Use for Reflection and Revising

After revising their own work, have writers choose readers for their work. Each reader uses a parallel rubric to rate the paper and then meets with the writer to discuss the ratings and the reasons behind them. By having the writer lead the discussion using the questions at the top, the discussion has the tone of curiosity on the part of the writer and of a helpful analysis by the reader, rather than a critique. We have used rubrics in digital environments, but the main benefit of the technology in this case is creating the document digitally so it can be easily edited, removing a significant barrier to using rubrics for feedback. Table 2.1 shows a writer's rubric and Table 2.2 shows a reader's rubric.

Reader's Rubric—What Makes My Writing Worth Reading?

Analyzing the Structure After the Fact

When students feel they are close to a final draft, have them exchange papers and have the reader create an outline of the paper. Students can use an outlining, mapping program such as *Inspiration* or web 2.0 tools such as http://gliffy.com or http://mindomo.com. Students can email the outlines to each other, copying you, or they can post them in a common folder. Then the original writers can compare this outline with their beginning outlines. This "second look" gives writers a new way to look at what they have written. It often results in students noticing redundancies or holes in what they have written. They realize they have left something out or that the balance of ideas doesn't represent what they wanted, which are issues they can easily resolve. Comparing these "second look" outlines to beginning outlines gives writers the chance to reflect on how the writing evolved, what they retained from their original outline, and where they diverged. This is an important step because it reinforces the idea that writing evolves and gives students confidence that they can work that way too. Using an outline after the fact also gives students a tool that lets them check the overall structure themselves.

In a fifth-grade class we worked with, the teacher was a big proponent of outlines. For at least a third of the students, creating an outline was new and fairly painful. It almost seemed to get in the way of their story writing. When we gave students the option of creating an outline before, during, or after writing a story about an adventure they would like to have in their own

Table 2.1 Writer's rubric

	Focus	Content	Organization	Style	Conventions
	What is the point of the story?	*What does the reader know from reading what I wrote?*	*How did I tell the story? How did I organize it?*	*What pictures did my writing paint in the reader's mind?*	*What do I need to proofread for?*
4 Fluid	The reader knows what my point is about the topic and why I think that.	I make my point by choosing the most interesting and important ideas to tell the reader in an interesting, fun way.	I chose to organize it the way I did to be interesting and easy to read.	People can tell that a piece of writing is mine by how I write.	Anyone can read and understand my writing because I use correct spelling, punctuation, and grammar.
3 Focused	I make one big point about the topic or idea in the prompt. There are a lot of smaller ideas to support the big idea.	I know what I am talking about and the reader does too after they read what I wrote. It makes my point.	I tell what I know like a story with a beginning, middle, and end connected with transition words.	My readers feel like I am talking to them and they are part of what is happening. I use lots of interesting words and phrases.	When I reread what I wrote, I corrected the spelling, punctuation, and grammar.
2 Organized	I chose ideas that go together and tell why I think they go together.	I collected a lot of ideas and used the best ones to make my point.	I thought about how to tell the story so it would make sense to the reader.	I write like I talk. I want readers to understand what I write.	I asked a classmate to read my writing and ask me questions about what wasn't clear to her.
1 Draft	I write some ideas about the topic that come into my mind as I write.	I write about some things I have heard about the topic.	I write down what I think in the order I think of it.	I tell what happened in just a few sentences.	I write a lot of ideas instead of complete sentences. I spell words like I hear them.

Non-scorable: blank, illegible, incoherent, insufficient | Off-prompt: readable but does not respond to prompt

Table 2.2 Reader's rubric

	Focus	Content	Organization	Style	Conventions
	What is the point of the story or essay?	*What do you know from reading what I wrote?*	*How did I begin? How did it develop? How does it end? How is it organized?*	*What pictures did my writing paint in your mind?*	*What do I need to proofread for?*
4 Fluid	I know what the point is about the topic and why you think that.	You make your point by choosing the most interesting and important ideas to tell the reader in an interesting, fun way.	You chose to organize it the way you did to make it interesting and easy to read.	People can tell that a piece of writing is yours by how you write.	Anyone can read and understand your writing because you use correct spelling, punctuation, and grammar.
3 Focused	You make one big point about the topic or idea in the prompt. There are a lot of smaller ideas to support the big idea.	You know what you are talking about and now I do too after I read what you wrote. It makes your point.	You tell what you know like a story with a beginning, middle, and end connected with transition words.	Your readers feel like you are talking to them, and they are part of what is happening. You use lots of interesting words and phrases.	When I reread what you wrote, I am not distracted by the spelling, punctuation and grammar.
2 Organized	You chose ideas that go together and tell why you think they go together.	You used your best ones to make your point.	You thought about how to tell the story so it would make sense to the reader.	You write like you talk. You clearly want readers to understand what you write.	You had someone read and edit for spelling, punctuation, and grammar.
1 Draft	You write some ideas about the topic.	You write about some things you have heard about the topic.	You seem to have written down what you think in the order you think of them.	You tell what happened in just a few sentences.	You write a lot of ideas instead of complete sentences. Many words are written like they sound.
Non-scorable: blank, illegible, incoherent, insufficient			Off-prompt: readable but does not respond to prompt		

"backyard," the resistance went away. One student wrote a story about a boy (himself) who created a network of ramps through the neighborhood for bikes and skateboards. He was a "no outline" student, but when he sat down to do it after writing his story, he realized he had left out the part about designing the network of ramps so he added that as a flashback during a daydream. He was very pleased with this addition and became a fan of outlining, even using it before writing to organize his thoughts sometimes.

Summarization as a Tool to Improve Writing Ability

Summarization involves explicitly and systematically teaching students how to summarize texts and has a strong effect on writing ability (effect size = .82; Graham & Perin, 2007b). Used as a study strategy for nonfiction, summarization involves teaching students "cues of importance," so their summaries refer to the web of ideas (Friend, 2000). Cues include the following:

- Centrality: An idea is important if it is referred to by other ideas. The more frequently the author refers to an idea in relationship to other ideas, the more important it is.
- Structural cues: Writers use paragraphs, chapters, and sections to "chunk" ideas so these structures have main ideas and support other larger ideas.
- Generalization: What general statement can they make that would include all those ideas in a paragraph or section? In the whole piece? Thinking about the label or category that the ideas might fit into helps identify the main ideas.
- Redundant information: Students delete (or cross out) redundant information, elaborations on ideas, examples, and visualizations, leaving the main ideas and important details.
- Keywords: Students list keywords in the order they appear in the text and then pare down the list to the keywords that capture the main idea.

CCSS Connection

- Write arguments to support claims in an analysis of substantive topics or texts, using valid reasoning and relevant and sufficient evidence.

Practice using these cues makes students more aware of the structure of ideas, the choices writers have, and the responsibility for being clear for the reader. They learn how to make repeated references to the most important ideas as they provide detail or introduce related ideas. Ideas are no longer seen as standing alone or being introduced and used without continuing to place them in the whole web of ideas that are presented. It is helpful to introduce students to text structures at some point, including enumeration, chronological order, compare and contrast, cause and effect, journalism's 5 Ws + H, and problem and solution.

Technology can greatly enhance the use of summaries. We recommend having students create summaries of their own or other students' writing. Students can create podcast summaries of each other's stories or essays; then you can post the podcasts on a website and have students vote on the best summary. The audio recording technology shifts the focus from writing the summary to creating it and reading it. The public display and multiple readers create an authentic audience. The author gets feedback that supports further refinement of the piece. A win-win here!

Using the redundant strategy on digital text, teams of two to four students read the same essay or story written by one of them. Independently, they use the highlight text tool to indicate redundancies, elaborations, examples, and other unnecessary language to reveal the main ideas to be included in the summary. Only new ideas get highlighted. When students compare their versions, looking specifically for commonalities, they identify the key ideas to use to summarize the passage. This strategy is particularly effective since the main ideas jump off the page with the highlighting. This is not unlike the way those key ideas stand out to the skilled reader, so the technology provides scaffolding toward developing that skill. Here is an example, in which the underlined words have been highlighted:

Four score and seven years ago our fathers brought forth, upon this continent, a <u>new nation</u>, conceived in Liberty, and dedicated to the proposition that <u>all men are created equal</u>. Now we are engaged in a great <u>civil war, testing whether that nation</u>, or any nation so conceived and so dedicated, <u>can</u> long <u>endure</u>. We are met here on a great battlefield of that war. We have come to dedicate a portion of it as a final resting place for those who here gave their lives that that nation might live. It is altogether fitting and proper that we should do this. But in a larger sense we can not dedicate—we can not consecrate—we can not hallow this ground. The brave men, living and dead, who struggled, here, have consecrated it far above our poor power to add or detract. The world will little note, nor long remember, what we say here, but can never forget what they did here. It is for us, the living, rather to be dedicated here to the unfinished work which they have, thus far, so nobly carried on. It is rather for us to be here dedicated to the great task remaining before us—that from these honored dead we take increased devotion to that cause for which they here gave the last full measure of devotion—that we here highly resolve that these <u>dead shall not have died in vain</u>; that this nation shall have a new birth of freedom; and that <u>this government</u> of the people, by the people, for the people, <u>shall not perish</u> from the earth.

(Retrieved April 1, 2009, from http://americancivilwar.com/north/lincoln.html)

Using visual mapping tools, students highlight keywords as they find them and then add connections with words or phrases on lines between the key ideas. Ideas without connections do not satisfy the centrality cue so they are eliminated or combined with other ideas. This strategy lets students list any keyword they want without a lot of deliberation, and those that end up with a lot of connections survive as keywords. Seeing all the connections to the ideas that are truly central helps students understand what a central idea is. As writers, they can use this strategy in reverse: mapping their ideas first, then writing from the map, and adding ideas back to the map to match the developing text. Favorite ideas that do not seem to fit can be "parked" on the side of the map until they can be woven into the text. Ideas that are thought of later in the writing process can be "back mapped" and then embedded in the text in the introduction, through foreshadowing or flashbacks, or in dialogue or sidebars. In nonfiction, connecting every idea to the central ideas helps students eliminate irrelevant ideas, use segues, and organize their ideas. Maps can be turned into outlines manually or, in the case of the program *Inspiration,* automatically. Here is an example of an excerpt from a story that was later mapped:

AT LUNCH, Todd thought of things he could sell. Everything he owned of any value, he could touch: his grandfather's watch, his grandmother's wedding ring, a gold necklace belonging to some forgotten relative. His car, too, but that was out of the question as he needed it to work.

He got up from his chair and scanned the floor below, the robots still working away, a sea of metallic shoulders rising and falling in unison, strangely beautiful in a way. Over by the forklift sat 8831, his eyes as blank as the piece of bread he was eating.

Two weeks from today was Todd's thirtieth wedding anniversary, and even if he were to pawn the watch, the ring, and the necklace, he knew he wouldn't even come close to having enough for Paris. That's where Sue had wanted to go for as long as he could remember. They didn't have the money to honeymoon there, but that was okay because back then, there had been plenty of time. They were young, both healthy and working, so they would save a little here and there and in a couple of years, they would be walking up to the Eiffel Tower at night arm in arm, find themselves underneath the arch and look up at the beacon that shined on this city of lights.

But then came two sons and three recessions and a second mortgage. A hysterectomy for her, a double bypass for him, and now here he was, nine years short of retirement, supervising a team of robots and a retarded man, thinking about folks who could sell things they couldn't touch, like stocks and bonds and whatever else he couldn't even fathom, people with money who would pay to experience another's most cherished moments. ("Paris at Night" by Sung J. Woo. Retrieved April 12, 2009 from www.short-stories.co.uk)

Figure 2.4 is a concept map of just this section of the short story. It evolved as the reader put the pieces together and began to relate them. You can see how a summary could be built from a map like this, with the key ideas being the ones with the most links that are central to the events.

To learn and practice using structural cues and generalization, have students create a single cell table for each chunk (paragraph, chapter, section). As they read, students jot down what they think are the main ideas in the box (Figure 2.5). At the end, they look back over the words and phrases, eliminate irrelevant or less important ideas that make generalizing difficult, and write a generalization about the words in the box. These generalizations can then be used to summarize the whole piece. We recommend having students use this strategy on their own or each other's writing. It then becomes a prewriting option to "block out" the main ideas and details for their future writing. We recommend using a spreadsheet because with "wraptext" formatting for cells, they expand to fit how much you write. More columns are available for additional reviews or notes.

Technology makes teaching and using the skill of summarizing versatile and interesting for students. The ease of moving, highlighting, and mapping text helps them develop the ability to identify main ideas in their own writing, eliminate irrelevant ideas, and weave the connections among ideas that make writing a powerful means of communication.

Paris at Night
blank eyes
sitting
30th wedding anniversary
8331 (retarded man)
car
grandfather's watch
thinking about
for
supervising
Everything he could sell
Todd working
gold necklace
wife Sue wants to go to Paris
supervising
grandmother's wedding ring
not enough to go to Pans
robots working
imagined
need money
walking arm in arm at night
cost money
strangely beautiful
expenses since married
two sons
second mortgage
3 recessions
medical expenses

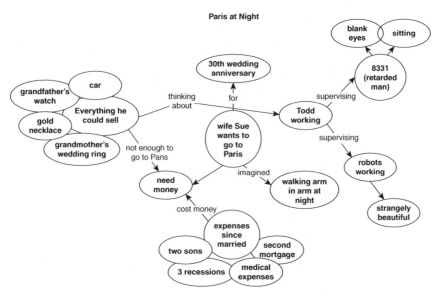

Figure 2.4 Concept map for a short story

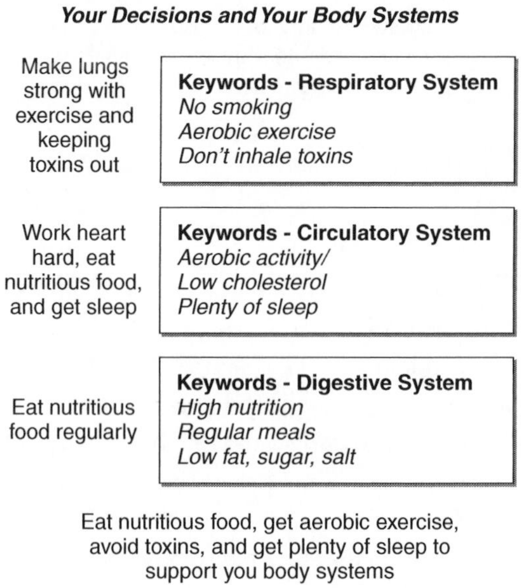

Your Decisions and Your Body Systems
Make lungs strong with exercise and keeping toxins out
Keywords - Respiratory System
No smoking
Aerobic exercise
Don't inhale toxins
Work heart hard, eat nutritious food, and get sleep
Keywords - Circulatory System
Aerobic activity/
Low cholesterol
Plenty of sleep
Eat nutritious food regularly
Keywords - Digestive System
High nutrition
Regular meals
Low fat, sugar, salt
Eat nutritious food, get aerobic exercise, avoid toxins, and get plenty of sleep to support you body systems

Figure 2.5 Main ideas chart

Sentence Combining

Sentence-combining instruction focuses on teaching students to construct more complex, sophisticated sentences to improve their writing. Compared with grammar instruction, sentence-combining instruction was more effective and showed moderate effects (effect size = .50, Graham & Perin, 2007b). Sentence combining, along with planning and revising, are the three major strategies skilled writers use (Hayes & Flower, 1986). Furthermore, difficulty in sentence construction

Table 2.3 Combining Simple Sentences

Simpler sentences	Combining Strategy	More complex sentences
Jury duty should be taken seriously. Citizens need to contribute to preserve the democratic process.	Use *and, but* or *because* to connect two related sentences into a compound sentence.	Citizens need to take jury duty seriously because it contributes to preserving the democratic process.
Listening to others makes them feel important. Asking questions lets people know you are listening. Eye contact is important in a conversation.	Combine ideas with commas into one sentence.	To have a good conversation, listen to the other person, make eye contact, and ask questions so they feel important.
Buying a new boat is an exciting, intensive process. Some people like buying boats.	Take a critical adjective or adverb from one sentence and put it into another.	Some people like buying boats because it is an exciting, intensive process.
Spring weather is wet and dry, hot and cold, windy and calm. It can be frustrating for planning outdoor activities.	Make the main idea of one sentence into an adjectival or adverbial clause and put it into another.	It can be frustrating to plan outdoor activities in the spring when the weather is wet and dry, hot and cold, and windy and calm.
Morning talk shows are popular. Some people like them for the interviews. Others like them for the jokes. Help with solving problems attracts some people.	Embed the key ideas from several sentences into one using clauses and phrases.	People like morning talk shows for their interviews, jokes, or help they provide in solving common problems.

may interfere with composing (Scardamalia & Bereiter, 1986; Strong, 1986). Students who are taught sentence-combining strategies have better papers than students who receive traditional grammar instruction (Saddler & Graham, 2005). To transfer the use of the strategies from exercises to be part of the revising process, suggest that students try some of these combining strategies shown in Table 2.3 as they revise their writing (adapted from Strong, 1986).

Upload this table in a word processor or spreadsheet, with the first and last columns blank for students to put in their own simple sentences, and then use the sentence-combining strategy to create a more complex sentence. Have students exchange files and suggest other alternative combinations. The new complex sentences can be copied to replace the simple sentences.

CCSS Connection

- Write informative/explanatory texts to examine and convey complex ideas and information clearly and accurately through the effective selection, organization, and analysis of content.

The theory is that knowing how to construct different kinds of sentences frees up mental activity to focus on the ideas, the organization, voice, and other aspects of the writing process (Graham,

1982). Sentence structure has also been shown to influence perceptions of writing quality (Freedman, 1979). Good complex sentences made readers think the writing is of a higher quality.

Technology tools provide a huge boost to writers in the drafting and revising stage of writing. The flexibility to try out ideas, structures, and models and to work collaboratively in shared spaces removes the barriers of rewriting and sharing paper copies.

Publishing

This stage of the writing process used to require students to make a final copy with their best handwriting and turn it in to the teacher. Thanks to an emphasis on "publishing" student writing for real audiences, some teachers helped students use special paper, encouraged them to illustrate their work, and then bind their books to put in the school library and be checked out by other students. Other teachers had students create newspapers or magazines that could be duplicated and shared with others. Technology now takes this one step further, making it possible to come much closer to the publication process for printed materials that was formerly reserved for only a few people. Students can insert graphics and pictures, use fonts and callouts, and create an overall layout to enhance the presentation and meaning of their writing.

We have noticed that students are much more interested in these visual features than are many adults. They choose them carefully and tinker with them until they are satisfied with the result. Their culture is more media based, so they have benefited from the incidental learning that has taken place through exposure. This exposure creates the desire and interest, but it may not be accompanied by an explicit understanding. In Chapters 7 and 8 we go into depth about how to teach students about these visual elements so they become discerning consumers and users. Here, let us consider how to structure assignments so students spend most of their time writing, and have some criteria for working on the visual presentation of that writing.

As in the other phases of the writing process, we recommend giving students time to work individually and then share their work and seek feedback from peers—revising based on that feedback. Based on the timeline for writing a piece, give students a schedule of intermediary deadlines that include the publishing "window." Table 2.4 shows an example.

Notice that publishing takes almost a third of the time. It is well worth it. Polishing a piece for publication serves several important functions. First and foremost, it honors the work of the writer by spending the time to make the presentation as good as possible. Second, it makes the writing more attractive and interesting so it is more likely to attract an audience. To feel like people want to read what they write is very motivating to some writers. If not motivating, it is at least appreciated by many writers. Third, it is another way for writers to step back from their work and see it

Table 2.4 Publishing schedule

Nov. 1–5	Idea generation and prewriting
Nov. 6–12	Drafting and revising
Nov. 17–21	Publishing

more objectively through its new format. This supports that habit of getting distance from the work throughout the process. At the publishing stage, it often evokes pride in the writer.

Perhaps the easiest place to get started is to have students choose a favorite piece of writing from the marking period to be published. This process of having students rework pieces of writing will show them they have become better writers over the course of the year. Once they have decided on a piece of writing and it has been edited, proofed, and readied, you need a place to publish their work. Traditionally, this was done by printing each work and then binding it into a book, often by hand. A decidedly more modern way to accomplish this is to have students submit their work to you, and then you send it in to an online company that binds the work professionally, complete with title page, covers, and an "about the author" section.

Give Students Specific Product Goals

Along with the timeline, consider giving students more detailed guidelines for their writing. When students are provided specific goals for their writing, they produce significantly better work (effect size = .70, Graham & Perin, 2007a). For example, to teach students strategies for how to write persuasively, ask them to provide reasons for their positions, sources, and opposing positions. Teach them what this means and provide them with some scaffolding to see the improvement. One way to use technology for this process is to begin with a discussion board around this prompt:

Think of a time you changed your mind.
Tell us about that time and what persuaded you to change your mind.

In class, use examples from the discussion threads of position statements, reasons, and evidence. Give students a visual template to organize their first draft around the elements of a good persuasive essay. Students produce better writing when they create organized drafts as opposed to a collection of notes or long composed drafts (Piolat & Roussey, 1996). For example, in writing a persuasive essay, students produce better essays when they work from an "elaborated goal" that explicitly uses the structure of stating a position, supporting it with reasons and evidence, and rebutting reasons of someone with an opposing position (Ferretti, MacArthur, & Dowdy, 2000).

Create a wiki or use another online space to store this template and examples of students' organized drafts. Continue to ask students to discuss the elements of persuasion for homework in the discussion board, and teach mini-lessons based on their questions and areas where they seem fuzzy. Questions for discussion include these:

- Why is a position statement based on what someone "believes" as opposed to what he or she thinks or feels? What's the difference?
- What makes a position statement clear?
- How do the reasons add up so they lead to the position statement?
- What makes some evidence better than other evidence?
- What makes some sources better than others?

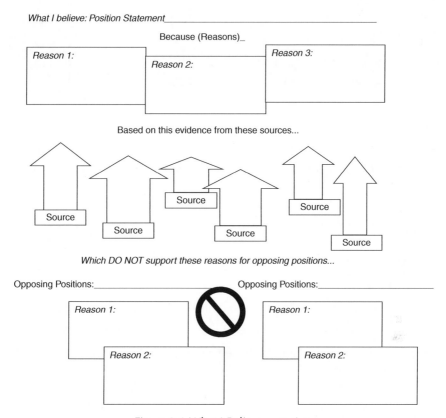

Figure 2.6 What I Believe organizer

Have these discussions online and in class the following day as students continue to write and revise. Use class time for them to write, revise, and review each other's drafts at least once or twice so you can see how they are applying what they are learning about the strategy and talk with them about it. Figure 2.6 shows an example.

Be sure to keep copies of their original drafts so they can see how far they have come. Improvements can fall through the cracks in a digital environment since drafts evolve so quickly. We recommend adding the date to the file name. Each time the students opens the document to edit it, have them "save as" with that day's date. Editors can add their initials before the date.

Cherish Audiences Throughout the Writing Process

As we have discussed, a writer may seek out an audience at any stage of the writing process to clarify his or her thinking, get feedback on a passage, or try out an idea. We are generally very protective of our ideas, even going so far as to screen out information that is contrary to what we think we know or believe. Called "cognitive dissonance" (Festinger, Riecken, & Schacter, 1956), this phenomenon can prevent us from getting helpful feedback or taking in ideas that are valuable. Building in feedback throughout the process develops the habit of seeing one's own writing through other's eyes. This trumps the tendency to be an audience of one.

CCSS Connection

- Produce clear and coherent writing in which the development, organization, and style are appropriate to task, purpose, and audience.

Challenge your students to write for specific publications or audiences. Since many magazines, e-zines, websites, and other publications have specific needs, interests, audiences, and style, have your students choose a publication to write for. Steps they might follow include these:

1. Analyze the publication; read several issues or pages for the style, author backgrounds, and topics.
2. Look for their publication guidelines to find out who they publish, upcoming themes, and what they are looking for in submissions.
3. Choose something you have written that you think would fit this publication's needs.
4. Shape your piece of writing to fit the publication and its audience.
5. Submit it with a letter to the editor about the research you did and why you think their publication meets their needs.

With the proliferation of online publications, many options are available. While self-publishing is still an option through blogs, wikis, e-books, and e-zines, some of your students may also want to investigate existing publications for their work.

The website http://giftedhandswriting.com offers resources for writing for online magazines. For example, your students may wish to write for younger children on a site such as www.dogonews.com. This site's purpose is to encourage younger children to read. It has regular contributors ages 9–14. There is a note on the website encouraging writers who are interested to contact the editor.

Stone Soup (www.stonesoup.com) publishes stories, poems, book reviews, and art of students 13 and younger. Submissions of up to 2,500 words must be printed and mailed. They also accept illustrators and reviewers and pay for work!

Teen Ink (www.teenink.com) is an online magazine students can subscribe to and be published in. Their submission guidelines require a writer to register and encourage 13–19-year-olds to submit their work (mostly 2,500 words or less). There are no deadlines, and Teen Ink has several publications, including a monthly print magazine and a poetry journal. They reserve the right to edit the teens' writing, unless they submit to *Teen Ink RAW* where the unedited submissions are published. On Teen Ink you will see reviews, opinion pieces, poetry, art/photos, fiction, and nonfiction.

Writing contests are another possibility for publication. The Poets & Writers site lists grants and awards at www.pw.org/grants?apage that are mainly for adults but might interest some of your students. Regardless of how your students "publish" their work, the process of preparing it in a final form will provide opportunities for valuable reflection and celebration.

Author's Chair

Author's Chair is a strategy developed by New Zealand educator Marie Clay. When a piece of writing is finished, having the author read parts of it aloud, answer questions from readers, and discuss his or her thinking can be a very positive experience. The purpose of this strategy is discussion, unlike the critique during the revising/editing stage. The author is treated as any published author would be, with respect and interest. He chooses a passage to read and sits facing the audience. The audience may or may not have read the work ahead of time, although we find that if they have already read it, the discussion is much richer. The audience makes positive comments about the writing. You can provide them with examples of how they might phrase their comments. Here are some examples:

- I like the way you described . . . because . . .
- What you wrote reminds me of . . .
- How you write makes me think of . . . (another writer)
- It's interesting to me that you . . . because . . .
- I notice that . . .

They may also ask questions, although they should not be challenging or critical questions, but rather more like these ones:

- Where did you get the idea for this work?
- Have you written other things like this?
- What was most surprising to you about how this piece turned out?
- Was this easy or difficult to write?
- Do you have other ideas based on this piece that you will pursue next?

Initially if you are doing this with your class, you will model the kind of comments and questions that are appropriate. When students are used to the model, you may want to have a student serve as moderator.

To support the Author's Chair with technology, video- or audiotape the discussion and post it online for others to enjoy and add their own comments. Tape it in a compressed form and turn off the camera between the comment and question sections to keep the size of the files manageable. Ask a student to write a press release about the author event and use that to introduce the audio or video clips on the site. This becomes an archive of student work that students can send to their family and friends and revisit as they continue to publish.

Blogging to Develop Voice

Blogging is another tool that students can use to jot down their thoughts and experiences. Designed primarily for personal expression, blogs can help your students develop a comfortable writing style and voice. These collections of thoughts and opinions, interests, and ideas become a rich source of writing ideas that students can relate to topics they are currently writing about or can even become full-blown essays or stories. They can be public or private, and accessed from anywhere.

Blogs are easy to set up for free. Each new entry appears with the date it was written. Old entries can be archived in the sidebar. Website links, pictures, and video links can be added. Students can take advantage of suggestions designed for professionals on how to write for blogs such as the following (adapted from Krakoff & Wakeman, n.d.):

- Write for the reader.
- Say something valuable.
- Proofread to show respect for your readers.
- Keep it simple—get to the point quickly.
- Use a lively, inviting style.
- Link often to show your place in the wider world of ideas.
- Use keywords often to keep on message and get more hits.
- Write clearly without jargon.
- Write the way you talk.
- Use a clear, bold headline for each entry.

Like the other stages of the writing process, publishing benefits greatly from technology tools. Writers have many more options for how to present their work and to whom. What they need from school is experience developing the mindset and processes that will help them make the most of the tools. Helping them to analyze the options, choose thoughtfully, and fully engage in the process is the role of the teacher in the classroom. The publishing stage is the time to relish the reaction of audiences, to shift from crafting to being curious about what people make of the work, and, most of all, getting it out there to be read! We've found Blogger to be the best free blogging website for this purpose. Teachers can take advantage of the blog's collaborative features by asking students to post comments and questions. For example, as part of a lesson on Shakespeare, you could post weekly passages from plays and ask students to reply (comment) with their "plain English" interpretations. You could also give them the easier option of paraphrasing the passage in their own words.

Using the Technology—Blogging (Blogger)

Blogger is a blogging tool you can use for free. Most blogging sites are designed similarly to this one. So, if you choose to use WordPress, LiveJournal, or any of the others, the directions will be slightly different, but the outcome will be the same—you will be blogging in no time.

Go to the Blogger.com homepage. Choose the "Get Started Here" link and complete the sign-up page. Once finished, choose the "New Blog" link, and Blogger will send a link to your email to activate your new blog. Figure 2.7 shows what the TechforLiteracy Blogger blog homepage looks like. Figure 2.8 shows the composing window.

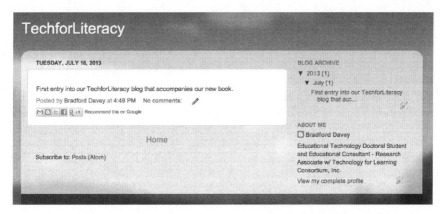

Figure 2.7 TechforLiteracy Blogger homepage

Figure 2.8 TechforLiteracy blog composition window

3 | Using Technology for Reading and Writing Projects

Ultimately reading and writing are tools for constructing knowledge. They are ways we learn from others, learn about ourselves, and share what we have learned, think, feel, and observe. Activities that explicitly challenge students to create and invent are given a boost from technology tools. As we have seen, whether reading for pleasure, reflecting, or writing for a specific purpose, technology opens up possibilities for how we read, compose, and publish. In this chapter, we discuss how to use technology for collaborative writing, the process approach to writing, inquiry activities, and portfolios.

Collaborative Writing

CCSS Connection

- Produce clear and coherent writing in which the development, organization, and style are appropriate to task, purpose, and audience.

- Write informative/explanatory texts to examine and convey complex ideas and information clearly and accurately through the effective selection, organization, and analysis of content.

An effective strategy for teaching writing is collaborative writing in which students work together to plan, draft, revise, and edit their compositions. Studies (Graham & Perin, 2007b) show strong positive effects on the quality of student writing (effect size = .75) of environments in which students help each other with one or more aspects of their writing. Collaborative writing has had more of an effect on writing quality than teacher corrections (Boscolo & Ascorti, 2004), grammar instruction (Olson, 1990), individual rewriting (Prater & Bermudez, 1993; Yarrow & Topping, 2001), or process writing instruction (MacArthur, Schwartz, & Graham, 1991).

Wikis provide a free collaborative writing environment in which there is a record of contributions and edits and the latest version is always "on top." Wikis support knowledge construction in three ways:

1. They move information students have learned more toward usable knowledge by having them collaborate to express what they think they have learned.

2. They involve everyone in the writing process; each person's contribution moves forward the group's and the individual's understanding as they negotiate and try out what they want to include. What each person thinks matters, and at the same time it must withstand the scrutiny of the group.

3. They provide a "product" of what students have learned, a form of evidence of learning for the students themselves that they can use to reflect on what and how they learned and also can share with others.

While the wiki provides the space for knowledge construction to occur, the guidance of the teacher in structuring the task is required (Reynard, 2009). Table 3.1 shows a variety of different collaborative strategies you can use to structure how students work together (based on a study conducted by Ede & Lunsford, 1990). You may also want to give students the choice of setting up the structure for how they work together based on the task and their preferences. What is most important is that they establish *how* they are going to work together so everyone knows what to expect and to do. Of course, as we have discussed, you can use other tools such as Google Docs for collaborative writing.

What makes collaborative writing positive and worthwhile? Ede and Lunsford (1990) examined the level of satisfaction of 800 writers in the collaborative writing process. Based on their findings, some useful guidelines for collaborative writing are given below. These are the things that led to high satisfaction with collaborative writing. We suggest you have students make a list of what would make them happy with collaborative writing and then give them the following list.

- Share your ideas openly and respectfully. Listen to others' ideas.
- Figure out the goal and state it as a group.

Table 3.1 Collaborative strategies

Collaborative strategy	Outlining Task	Drafting	Editing	Publishing
Multiple separate writers	Group	Each member does her part	Group compiles parts	One or two of the writers
One writer, multiple editors	Writer	Writer	Writer	One member
Writer and editors work independently	Writer	Writer	Editors without consulting writer	One member
Multiple writers work independently of editors	Group of writers	Group of writers	Editors without consulting writer	One editor
One planner/editor, multiple writers	One planner	Writers	Editor	Editor
One writer, one editor	Writer	Writer	Editor	Editor

- Decide how credit will be shared (order of authors—alphabetical, most work, other).

- Discuss how you will deal with disagreements when they arise.

- Set up a timeline.

- Discuss who is doing what so you share control of the text.

- Respond to both things you agree with and things you don't.

- Discuss and agree on whom to share the results with together.

You can have students use these guidelines to discuss how they are working together throughout the process. If you are having students work in a wiki, Google Doc, or other collaborative space, put these guidelines in each group's folder and set regular times for them to rate how they are working together as a group on a scale of 1–10. Each student should rate how things are going in the group for them individually and then share their ratings. The group can make adjustments and continue to be productive.

Google Docs (docs.google.com) offer coauthored collaborative document creation in real time. Students can also create spreadsheets and presentations and upload their current work not created in Google. They will recognize the standard interface as it is very similar to word processing software. Once a student authors a document, he or she shares it with others by inviting them to join. Editing can take place from anywhere there is Internet access, and the student's work is safely stored. We recommend you have students also invite you to view their documents to allow you to monitor student progress and track changes over time in their thinking and reasoning. The first image (Figure 3.1) is from the Google Docs homepage. It shows the basic instructional guide for becoming a document author, inviting others, and editing work.

This second image (Figure 3.2) is a screen capture of a document created by three authors— one living in California, the second in Rhode Island, and the third in São Paulo, Brazil. Although separated by great distance, the three were able to collaboratively work on a graduate school assignment.

The third image (Figure 3.3) can be found by clicking on the file tab at the top of the page and then choosing "Document History." It shows a historical record of each time the document

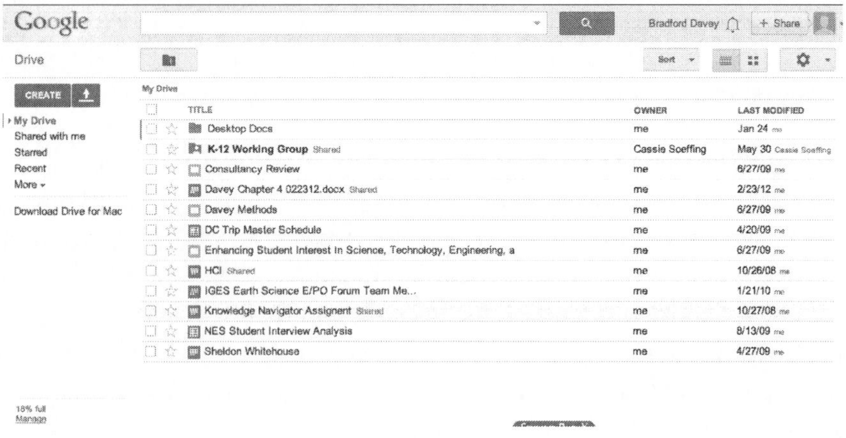

Figure 3.1 Google Docs

Figure 3.2 Screen capture of collaborative writing

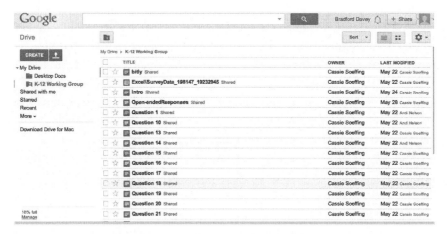

Figure 3.3 Google Docs—document history

was opened by one of the team members and what changes, edits, or additions were made. In this example, 73 revisions were made to the document by a team of three over a period of three weeks. It is often difficult to get students to do one revision to their own work, but tracking those changes and working with others can be motivational.

Collaborative writing adds another level of discussion and reflection to the writing process, causing the group members to inquire into their own motivations and actions in writing as well as observing what others do. This additional level of reflection and discussion can be very positive if each member contributes and the ground rules are clear. The technology makes it easy to work and rework pieces, discuss directions and phrasing, and polish a piece asynchronously, all outside of class. We recommend giving groups some class time daily to discuss their progress and iron out any issues that have arisen, check in on the timeline, and discuss next steps.

Process Writing Approach

Throughout section one of this book, we have taken a process writing approach, treating the teaching of writing as a process that can be taught. We have encouraged you to use the informal reading and writing students do as grist for their writing mill, feeding it with ideas and creating conversations among students about their writing. Before the process approach was used, students were taught grammar and vocabulary development and were then given writing assignments that were graded by the teacher. There was little attention to intervening in the writing process done by individuals since it was believed that if you corrected their writing, they would transfer what they learned from those corrections to their next writing assignment. Unfortunately, this was not the case. Teachers were spending lots of time correcting writing errors that appeared again and again. In the 1970s, the process of writing, as described by writers, began to be studied by educational researchers and teachers of writing, who then proposed to teach students strategies for the different phases of the writing process (Calkins, 1983, 1994; Emig, 1971; Flower & Hayes, 1977, 1980; Graves, 1983; Murray, 1980). Research since then has shown that teaching students about the process of writing, its recursive nature, and different strategies for each stage actually does improve writing. In a meta-analysis of rigorous research studies, Graham and Perin (2007b) found a small, but significant overall effect of the process approach (.32). The effect increased to .46 when teachers had specific training (Nagin, 2003). Not surprisingly, when students were more involved in analyzing and improving their writing, they transferred those skills and strategies to their next piece of writing. Graham and Perin (2007b) define the process writing approach as follows:

> The process writing approach involves a number of interwoven activities, including creating extended opportunities for writing; emphasizing writing for real audiences; encouraging cycles of planning, translating, and reviewing; stressing personal responsibility and ownership of writing projects; facilitating high levels of student interactions; developing supportive writing environments; encouraging self-reflection and evaluation; and offering personalized individual assistance, brief instructional lessons to meet students' individual needs, and, in some instances, more extended and systematic instruction. (p. 19)

Technology creates the opportunity for supporting the individual process of writing in the social context of the classroom, thereby facilitating learning to write and writing to learn. Consider an example of a science teacher using technology for writing:

> Janet teaches science. She took a reading and writing in the content areas workshop years ago; then last year she took a technology class. She already had students writing in response to reading, keeping double-entry journals, posting questions on the board to be answered through discussion, and writing answers in their learning logs. She already had them researching scientists and science topics and doing collaborative writing. But technology changed everything. She discovered Google groups, a web

tool for organizing content and people. With each student signed up for a free Google account, she could create a Google group for each class, post assignments, establish timelines, create discussion areas, and list resources. Each student could post her own notes, works in progress, questions to be answered, questions with answers, pieces in need of revising, and polished pieces. They each could have a private space with their "stuff" and be a member of the class and of other groups for collaborative writing or editing. This virtual environment mirrors the classroom writing activities and eliminates the difficulty of keeping track of paper copies, sharing the latest versions, and coordinating individual and group activities.

The use of technology for process writing eases the management of the writing, but more importantly, it sets up an environment that respects the individual as a writer and thinker. It mitigates against taking all students through the same set of steps, and instead encourages them to use the group feedback and class instruction to develop their own writing in their own way.

Inquiry Activities

Inquiry activities that have students write about something they have experienced have been found to have a positive effect on their writing (effect size = .32, Graham & Perin, 2007b). In their meta-analyses of the research, Graham and Perin (2007b, p. 19) define inquiry as follows:

> Effective inquiry activities in writing are characterized by a clearly specified goal (e.g., describe the actions of people), analysis of concrete and immediate data (observe one or more peers during specific activities), use of specific strategies to conduct the analysis (retrospectively ask the person being observed the reason for a particular action), and applying what was learned (assign the writing of a story incorporating insights from the inquiry process).

The idea is to help students enhance their experience through honing their observational skills to collect immediate data. They are urged to revisit the situation, delve more deeply into the data, or see the situation from multiple perspectives or over a period of time. The intensity of the experience provides rich details that are worthy of writing about. Such situations often inspire writers, and are the business of journalists.

Consider staging a harmless dramatic event. Someone bursts into the room, ostensibly looking for something frantically and asking lots of questions, and then just as suddenly leaves the room. Have each student write a description of what happened and then compare descriptions by quickly passing them to the next person. Discuss how data collection occurs by individual observers and how to prepare for more systematic data collection. Have them build a story around the event by developing the character, motive, and outcome.

CCSS Connection

● Use technology, including the Internet, to produce and publish writing and to interact and collaborate with others.

We like to then ask students to take this activity into the field. Have students use multiple technology tools: photo cameras, video cameras, sound recorders, measuring devices, georeferencing tools, and probeware (for example, pH, temperature). Ask them to collect data on the events and people at one location in the school over a period of five minutes from as many perspectives as possible and then to write a description based on the data. (If taking your students outside presents a safety issue in your school situation, have students collect data within the classroom.) If students have iPod touches, iPhones, or other mobile computing devices, they can collect most of these data right on them. We recommend having them work in groups of two or three to collect the data and write about it. Using collaborative writing, they can write from different perspectives or write up different aspects of their observations. They can include the photos and other data they collected. The only requirement is that they base everything on the data. So, picture this—five teams of your students observe and record data from the five minutes before school starts. Challenge them to look for ambiguous or emotional data such as a look of concern on the face of a student at her locker; a student standing, looking around and shifting back and forth; or a parent dropping a student off whose gaze lingers as her child walks away from the car.

Post all the pieces in a shared folder or online workspace so everyone in the class can read them, or have them read them aloud one by one. Have the listeners (or readers) identify commonalities in content and process. Use the following questions to guide the students in their analyses:

● Is there anything that everyone wrote about?

● Is there something that only one group wrote about?

● Did everyone take pictures? What other kinds of data were commonly collected?

● What data source was unique to only one group?

● Does the data seem believable or did the data present a distorted picture of the location and events?

For homework, ask each student to write about what he or she learned about using observation as the basis for writing by addressing these questions: What makes writing about observations worth reading? How do writers use their observation of life in their writing? How will you observe differently in the future? How will you incorporate observation into your writing?

Inquiry activities using technology may encourage some of your students to be more observant and to see the possibilities all around them. As Frank Smith observes, "Writing is for stories to be read, books to be published, poems to be recited, plays to be acted, cartoons to be labeled, instructions to be followed, designs to be made, recipes to be cooked, diaries to be collected . . . Writing is for ideas, action, interaction, and evidence" (1986, p. 179, cited in Calkins, 1994).

Portfolios of Reading and Writing

Digital portfolios provide a ready tool for students to reflect on what they have learned and show-case it. The best digital portfolios are those that are an integral part of the learning process. They capture the waves of action and reflection that characterize the learning process. On this digital canvas, the results and the processes of learning are intertwined through ongoing reflection.

CCSS Connection

- Use technology, including the Internet, to produce and publish writing and to interact and collaborate with others.

- Gather relevant information from multiple print and digital sources, assess the credibility and accuracy of each source, and integrate the information while avoiding plagiarism.

Digital portfolios (Figure 3.4) have all the benefits of physical portfolios, but also face some of the same challenges. They can be collections without reflection. They can be produced in isolation rather than as part of a learning community. They can be created as reports on learning, rather than being the part of the learning process that reveals what was learned and how the learning occurred. Portfolios need a supportive culture such as process writing to be successful and valued by the students. When they work, teachers and students become more reflective and focused on the relationship of the learning activities to outcomes. Several factors are involved in the successful use of digital portfolios:

- Process orientation
- Multiple audiences
- Multiple media for expression
- Individual pacing
- Teamwork
- Technology

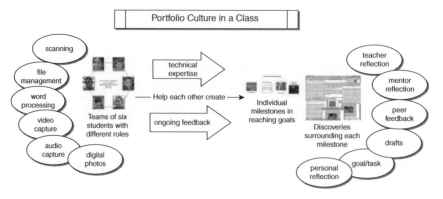

Figure 3.4 Digital portfolios

Process Orientation

The portfolio can be used to focus students on capturing the milestones in the process rather than getting it done. In a recent writing portfolio project we did, one of the teachers commented, "They just want to get it done, so they can record it," without improving it along the way. We recommend capturing the drafts at many different stages to heighten the importance of each draft and the improvement made in each. This shifts the focus from the final product to each stage along the way. As this shift occurred in that recent project, students began to see each stage as a way to learn and improve what they were doing—"to get ideas to make it better," as one student put it. They began to talk about the process for each milestone as "taking time" and used phrases like "I'm working on it" and "it is getting better all the time." Teachers commented on how this emphasis on revision was new and a welcome change. Because we used a different technology tool at each stage, students were motivated to reach each stage. We recommend starting with tools to brainstorm and organize ideas. We like *Inspiration* because it is *so* easy to use, but there are other Web 2.0 tools. If you only have a few computers in your class, set up a folder with writing tools and have students work independently. Others may do this at home.

Multiple Audiences

The multiple levels of audience—*self* as the milestones are created and recorded, *peers* as the writing is discussed, the *teacher* on request, or a *parent* after the writing is uploaded—support refinement of the products. Particularly in the writing portfolio classroom, the teacher may find the students are much more likely to use the strategies they have been taught in their writing in order to improve it from draft to draft. They begin listening to each other and using the language of writing to describe their work. For example, students begin to recognize why their stories are not interesting: "It needs a better beginning" or "it just stops." And they begin to talk about the strategies they use that have worked: "I like to use dialogue because it is interesting to hear people talk." Or, "I said her dress was as blue as the night sky so you would see it in your mind when you read it. I like to use analogies." As they become better able to talk about their motives, strategies, and needs, they offer and seek out help from each other.

Multiple Media for Expression

Using multiple media can also increase students' engagement with writing. They are more likely (and able) than before to "do their best" at each stage of the process when they get different perspectives on it. For example, when students can orally reflect on their drawings or writing, they can often elaborate about what they were thinking and what they intended in the piece. A videotaped interview by a fellow student can lead to further refinement. Students can coach each other to "speak up," "stay on the topic," "think about what you are going to say first." After making audio or video recordings, students can immediately review and discuss them and decide whether or not to redo them and what they learned that they can use in their next revision.

Individual Pacing

Developing a portfolio is a personal journey. It lays plain the work and thinking of the individual. Just like in the writing process itself, students have their own pace, style, and needs for creating and maintaining a portfolio. While it is important to respect this, we recommend you have minimum guidelines for what should be included and how often students contribute. For example, here are some guidelines:

- A sample from each stage of the writing process
- Feedback from at least two people in different forms (written, audio, video) during the revising stage
- At least one recorded interview of the writer
- The final piece
- Reflection on the final piece

Teamwork

Students need ways to interact around their writing—to get feedback from peers in different formats, be interviewed about their work at different stages, and seek out those whose writing they admire. If they are constantly sharing their writing, they become resources to each other. A student will seek out another student whose writing he admires. For example, a student in the writing portfolio project wanted to know where Sebastian got his ideas when given a writing prompt. While everyone else was making idea webs, doodling, brainstorming, or free writing to get started, Sebastian would sit—looking at his keyboard, looking out the window, looking at the ceiling—and then 10 or 15 minutes later, Sebastian would start writing and he wouldn't stop until he was finished. Jorge wanted to know what was going on in that first 10 minutes that let Sebastian write like that. Sebastian agreed to rewind his thinking and share it with Jorge. What Jorge discovered was that Sebastian's mind was racing with possibilities until he could see how a story would end. He couldn't map all those ideas; there were simply too many. And for him, it was a needle in a haystack problem, searching for an ending. When he had it, then he could write. Jorge realized he wasn't letting himself explore enough possibilities, and when he subsequently did, it not only improved his writing but he also had much more fun planning it. He also had not thought backward from amending. He wasn't sure how to do that yet, but he started paying a lot more attention to endings and how a story got there.

Technology

To create digital portfolios, students need easy access to word processing, scanning tools, cameras, and audio recording tools. These make the process interesting, giving students new perspectives on their writing and ways to interact around it.

Portfolios can be constructed using portfolio programs, Web 2.0 tools, or Google Docs. What is important is the process of collecting artifacts of the learning process all along the way, interacting with others, and reflecting on final products and what was learned.

Summary of Section I

This section has explored technology for reading and writing. The tools bring flexibility and creativity to the reading and writing processes. They create excitement and yet encourage greater discipline in producing quality work. While they emphasize the individual with all his or her idiosyncrasies, they also place the work in the context of the wider world and potential audiences for student thinking.

Key ideas

- Reading and writing are reciprocal.
- Technology aids reading through read-alongs, connecting to geography, providing aids for vocabulary and other concepts through links, access to reviews and annotations, note-taking for reading nonfiction, and finding back stories and context.
- Technology supports writing through word processing, templates for different kinds of writing (presentation tools, templates in Word), outlining (*Inspiration*), publishing (printing, blogs), group writing (wikis), and publishing for others to read.

References for Section I

Barnett, M. A. (1988). Reading through context: How real and perceived strategy use affects L2 comprehension. *The Modern Language Journal, 72,* 155–162.

Bennett, D. T. (1997, March/April). Providing role models online. *Electronic Learning, 19*(5), 50–51.

Bereiter, C., & Scardamalia, M. (1987). *The psychology of written composition.* Hillsdale, NJ: Lawrence Erlbaum Associates.

Bierema, L. L., & Merriam, S. B. (2002). eMentoring: Using computer mediated communication to enhance the mentoring process. *Innovative Higher Education, 26*(3), 211–227.

Boscolo, P., & Ascorti, K. (2004). Effects of collaborative revision on children's ability to write understandable narrative texts. In L. Allal, L. Chanquoy, & P. Largy (Eds.), *Revision: Cognitive and instructional processes.* In Rijlaarsdam, G. (Ed.). *Studies in writing,* Vol. 13 (pp. 157–170), Dordrecht, the Netherlands: Kluwer.

Brown. R. (1989). *Starting from Scratch: A Different Kind of Writiers; Manual.* New York: Bantam.

Calkins, L. M. (1983). *Lessons from a child: On the teaching and learning of writing.* Portsmouth, NH: Heinemann.

Calkins, L. M. (1994). *The art of teaching writing.* Portsmouth, NH: Heinemann.

Carvin, A. (2009). *Mobcasting the news: Crowdsourcing and journalism*. Paper presented at Digital Now Conference, Orlando, FL. Retrieved April 16, 2009, from www.scribd.com/doc/14258453/Mobcasting-the-News-Digitalnow-Conf-Carvin.

Dalton, D. W., & Hannafin, M. J. (1987). The effects of word processing on written composition. *Journal of Educational Research, 80,* 338–342.

De La Paz, S., & Graham, S. (2002). Explicitly teaching strategies, skills, and knowledge: Writing instruction in middle school classrooms. *Journal of Educational Psychology, 94,* 291–304.

Dillon, S. (2008). In test, few students are proficient writers. *New York Times*. Retrieved online from www.nytimes.com/2008/04/03/education/03cnd-writing.html?_r=0

Ede, L., & Lunsford, A. (1990). *Singular texts/plural authors: Perspectives on collaborative writing*. Carbondale, IL: Southern Illinois University Press.

Emig, J. (1971). *The composing processes of twelfth graders* (Research Rep. No. 13). Urbana, IL: National Council of Teachers of English.

Feldt, R., Byme, K., & Bral, C. (1996). Use of guided design to facilitate strategic reading. *Reading Improvement, 33,* 136–142.

Ferretti, R. P., MacArthur, C. A., & Dowdy, N. S. (2000). The effects of an elaborated goal on the persuasive writing of students with learning disabilities and their normally achieving peers. *Journal of Educational Psychology, 92,* 694–702.

Festinger, L., Riecken, H. W., & Schachter, S. (1956). *When prophecy fails*. Minneapolis: University of Minnesota Press.

Flower, L., & Hayes, J. R. (1977). Identifying the organization of writing processes. In L. W. Gregg & E. R. Steinberg (Eds.), *Cognitive processes in writing* (pp. 87–112). Hillsdale, NJ: Lawrence Erlbaum Associates.

Flower, L., & Hayes, J. R. (1980). Problem-solving strategies and the writing process. *College English, 39,* 449–461.

Freedman, S. (1979). How characteristics of student essays influence teachers' evaluations. *Journal of Educational Psychology, 71,* 328–338.

Friend, R. (2000). Teaching summarization as a content area strategy. *Journal of Adolescent & Adult Literacy, 44*(4), 320–329.

Graham, S. (1982). Composition research and practiced: A unified approach. *Focus on Exceptional Children, 14,* 1–16.

Graham, S., & Perin, D. (2007a). A meta-analysis of writing instruction for adolescent students. *Journal of Educational Psychology, 99*(3), 445–476.

Graham, S., & Perin, D. (2007b). *Writing NEXT: Effective strategies to improve writing of adolescents in middle and high schools*. New York: Carnegie Corporation.

Graves, D. H. (1983). *Writing: Teachers and children at work*. Portsmouth, NH: Heinemann.

Guetzloe, E. (1997). *The Power of Positive Relationships: Mentoring Programs in the School and Community. 41*(3), 27–44.

Harris, K., & Graham, S. (1996). *Making the writing process work: Strategies for composition and self-regulation*. Cambridge, MA: Brookline Books.

Hayes, J. R., & Flower, L. S. (1986). Writing research and the writer. *American Psychologist, 41,* 106–113.

Jones, S., & Fox, S. (2009). *Generations online in 2009.* Pew Internet & American Life Project. Retrieved March 1, 2009, from www.pewinternet.org/Reports/2009/Generations-Online-in-2009.aspx.

Karchmer, R. A. (2000, September). Using the Internet and children's literature to support interdisciplinary instruction. *Reading Teacher, 54,* 100–104.

Kiewra, K. (1998). A review of note-taking: The encoding-storage paradigm and beyond. *Educational Phychology Review, 1*(2), 147–161.

Kobayashi, K. (2007a). The Influence of critical reading orientation on external strategy use during expository text reading. *Educational Psychology, 27,* 363–375.

Krakoff, P., & Wakeman, D. (n.d.). *Top 10 blog writing tips.* Retrieved from http://website101.com/RSS-Blogs-Blogging/blog-writing-tips.html.

Lenhart, A., Arafeh, S., Smith, A., & Macgill, A. R. (2008). *Writing, technology and teens.* Pew Internet & American Life Project. Retrieved April 24, 2008, from www.pewinternet.org/Reports/2008/Writing-Technology-and-Teens.aspx.

Lipson, M. Y., & Wixson, K. K. (2003). *Assessment and instruction of reading and writing disability* (3rd ed.). New York: Longman.

Loretta, K. (2002). Technology as a Tool for Literacy in the Age of Information: Implications for the ESL Classroom. *Teaching English in the Two-Year College, 30*(2), 129–144.

MacArthur, C., Schwartz, S., and Graham, S. (1991). Effects of reciprocal peer revision strategy in special education classrooms. *Learning Disabilities Research and Practice, 6,* 201–210.

Marino, M. (2008). *Understanding How Adolescents with Reading Difficulties Utilize Technology-Based Tools.* New York: Routledge.

McKoen, R. (1941). *The Basic Works of Aristotle.* New York: Random House.

McLuhan, M. (1952). *The Mechanical Bride: Folklore of Industrial Man.* New York: Vanguard.

McLuhan, M., & Fiore, Q. (1967). *The medium is the message: An inventory of effects.* New York: Bantam Books.

McNabb, M. (2005). *Literacy learning in networked classrooms.* New York: International Reading Association.

Murray, D. M. (1980). Writing as process: How writing finds its own meaning. In T. R. Donovan & B. W. McClelland (Eds.), *Eight approaches to teaching composition* (pp. 3–20). Urbana, IL: National Council of Teachers of English.

Nagin, C. (2003). *Because writing matters: Improving student writing in our schools.* San Francisco: Jossey-Bass.

Newman, J. (1984). Language learning and computers. *Language Arts, 61*(5), 494–497.

Olson, R. (1990). Talking about text: How literacy contributes to thought. *Journal of Pragmatics, 14*(5), 705–721.

Palinscar, A. S., & Brown, A. L. (1984). Reciprocal teaching of comprehension-fostering and comprehension-monitoring activities. *Cognition and Instruction, 2*(1), 117–175.

Peverly, S. T., Brobst, K. E., Graham, M., & Shaw, R. (2003). College adults are not good at self-regulation: A study on the relationship of self-regulation, note taking, and test taking. *Journal of Educational Psychology, 95*(2), 335–346.

Piolat, A., & Roussey, J. (1996). Students' drafting strategies and text quality. *Learning and Instruction, 6*(2), 111–129.

Prater, D., & Bermudez, A. (1993). Using peer response groups with limited English proficient writers. *Bilingual Research Journal, 17*, 99–116.

Reynard, R. (2009). Why wikis? *T.H.E. Journal*. Retrieved online form www.thejournal.com/the/printacticle/?id=24279.

Robert, T., & Billings, L. (2009). Speak up and listen. *National Paideia Center*. Obtained from http://files.eric.ed.gov/fulltext/ED513482.pdf.

Robinson, F. P. (1941). *Diagnostic and remedial techniques for effective study*. New York: Harper Brothers.

Saddler, B., & Graham, S. (2005). The effects of peer-assisted sentence-combining instruction on the writing performance of more and less skilled young writers. *Journal of Educational Psychology, 97*, 43–54.

Sanchez, B., & Harris, J. (1996). *Online mentoring: A success story. Learning and Leading with Technology*. Retrieved from http://figg.handy4class.com/emissary/LLT_May_96.pdf

Scardamalia, M., & Bereiter, C. (1986). Research on written composition. In M. C. Wittrock (Ed.), *Handbook of research on teaching* (3rd ed., pp. 778–803). New York: Macmillan.

Schlozman, S. C., & Schlozman, V. R. (2000). Chaos in the classroom: Looking at ADHD. *Educational Leadership, 58*(3), 28–33.

Simic, M. (1994). *Computer assisted writing instruction*. ERIC Digest. Retrieved December 2011 from www.ericdigests.org/1995-2/computer.htm.

Smith, F. (1998). *The book of learning and forgetting*. New York: Teachers College Press.

Stauffer, R. G. (1969). *Directing reading maturity as a cognitive process*. New York: Harper & Row.

Strong, W. (1986). *Creative approaches to sentence combining*. ERIC No. ED274985. Urbana, IL: Urbana, IL: National Conference on Research in English/ERIC Clearinghouse on Reading and Communications Skills.

Sun, T., Youn, S., Wu, G., & Kuntaraporn, M. Online word-of-mouth (or mouse): an exploration of its antecedents and consequences. *J Comput-Mediat Commun 2006;11*(4) [http://jcmc.indiana.edu/vol11/issue4/sun.html].

Tolkien, J. R. R. (1955). *English and Welsh*. Retrieved April 9, 2009, from http://druidry.org/board/photos/englishandwelsh.pdf.

Topping, D., & McManus, R. (2002). *Real reading, real writing: Content–area strategies*. New York: Heinemann.

Valmont, W. J. (2003). *Technology for literacy teaching and learning*. Boston: Houghton Mifflin.

Yarrow, F., & Topping, K. (2001). Collaborative writing: The effects of metacognitive prompting and structured peer interaction. *British Journal of Psychology, 71*(2), 261–282.

Speaking and Listening

The simple lesson teachers seem to forget is that learning to communicate is learning to think.
—Terry Robert and Laura Billings, 2009

Key ideas

- Speaking and listening are how we communicate first and most often, even after we learn to read and write.

- Speaking allows some students to present their ideas more completely and fluently than writing.

- Audio recording of speech allows the listener to hear all of the aspects of speech and the speaker to capture it for themselves to review and improve on.

- Audio-captured speeches or conversations can become the basis for reading and writing.

- Speaking and listening are a medium for critical thinking.

- Technology tools for speaking and listening support individual differences in learning by offering multiple methods of presentation, expression, and engagement.

- Listening to lyrics can involve students in understanding characters, themes, and cultures.

- Listening to recorded stories or texts engages some students better than reading.

- Listening to others gives students a opportunity to connect, engage, and collaborate.

- Creating recordings for sharing with a wider audience can encourage students to refine their ideas and expression.

Research on Speaking and Listening

Speaking and listening have been identified as 21st-century skills by the U.S. Department of Education, the Partnership for 21st Century Skills, 21st Century Workforce Commission, and the National Alliance of Business and in multiple workplace readiness discussions. Speaking and listening enable students to approach complex problems with others and learn how to use critical thinking skills in conjunction with other minds.

How do students develop speaking and listening skills? Students improve their skills through active engagement in meaningful activities that require use of those skills. These activities can be organized around problems and solutions (sequential), causes and results (chronological), and similarities and differences (thematic; Wallace, Stariha, & Walbert, 2004). Speeches can be developed for specific situations and audiences so students have opportunities to adapt their speech to different situations. The classroom can be a place for students to practice their speaking skills and even experiment with different styles, intonations, volume, and pacing to take risks and push beyond their own limits (Perry, 2011).

As core as speaking and listening are to everyday existence, they have been described as transient and fleeting (Adler, 1983) and hence difficult to measure. Analyzing examples of students' writing over time is a clear and direct way to measure progress. Listening to conversations between two or more students presents a challenge to systematic assessment. However difficult to assess, the importance of speaking and listening for clear thinking, working and learning with others, and communicating ideas is clear.

Learning to speak and listen well is a long and challenging process, taking repeated practice and exposure. In this section, we discuss the importance of speaking and listening in learning, and present ideas for utilizing technology to enhance the learning process of developing skills and comfort in those areas.

Section Sections

Chapter 4: Technology Tools for Speaking

- Think Alouds
- Recording-Assisted Reading
- Partner Reading
- Call and Response
- Choral Reading
- Retelling
- Speech Making

Chapter 5: Technology Tools for Listening

- One-Way Communication
- Interactive Communication
- Listening to learn
- Assessment
- Active Listening
- Listening to Learn
- Differentiating with Sound (Amplification, Headsets)

Chapter 6: Using Technology for Speaking and Listening

- Readers Theater
- Verbal Dueling

- A New Take on Penpals
- Study Guides
- Improvisation and Role Playing

Speaking

Gesture, facial expression, and raw emotion are the first forms of communication we use to get our needs met, to connect with others, and to react to the world. Gradually, spoken words are added to this repertoire. We learn to mimic the sounds others make, then connect meaning to them, and eventually string words together to communicate. Gestures, facial expression, and intonation combine with the spoken word to provide meaning, nuance, and importance to the communication. Mehrabian (1971) found that, in communication of attitudes and feelings, listeners got 7% of the meaning from the words, 38% from the way the words were said, and 55% from the facial expression of the person.

Just as developmentally we first learn to speak, and use that oral communication for many years before learning to write, the oral traditions of cultures preceded their written documents by many thousands of years. Oral communication was used to pass on wisdom, help people solve problems, convey the law and social norms, and entertain. People relied on this communication and developed techniques to enhance it and preserve important ideas over time. With the coming of writing there was great concern that people's speaking and listening, memory, and organizing skills would atrophy. Without the discipline of giving and listening to speeches, some people argued, the mind would become lazy and unable to organize and remember complex ideas. While reading and writing have certainly overtaken speaking and listening as the core of taught literacy skills, speaking and listening still dominate most people's lives, and they need to be systematically developed. This instruction can build on the great oral traditions of the past while accommodating the technologies of today.

With the advent of digital tools, multimedia and virtual reality push us into richer forms of communication as they combine the spoken word with images and text to more closely resemble oral communication with its rich context of intonation and facial expression. We may be returning to something more like an oral tradition. "Like virtual reality, the power of the oral tradition emerges from the art of the narrative, which flows from nonliteral images and the call to participate. *This is not new wisdom, it is neglected wisdom* . . . In oral cultures, nonliteral imagination, feeling, and power intimately required each other . . . With ancient oral cultures, the narrative experience was an aesthetic experience" (Hohstadt & Keast, 2009). As students embrace new technologies, their imaginations are given voice through multiple media that evoke emotion and convey the power of their message.

What are the types of communication? Categories include intrapersonal communication or self-talk; interpersonal communication that can be one-way, interactive, or collaborative; group communication such as work or study groups that have a purpose or common interest; interviewing; and public speaking. Communications have a context (where and when they take place), a medium (method), a source that encodes or creates the message, and one or more receivers who decode it. Communicators get feedback, and both encoders and decoders can experience interference during the communication. Good communicators are made through preparation, practice, and presentations (Schwartzman, 2010). The goal is to have students understand the complexity, importance, and factors involved in human communication (Seeley-Case, 2010) and learn how to organize their thoughts, think critically about a topic, communicate about it clearly, use evidence to support any claims, become fluent in oral communication, gauge the effects of their speaking on audiences, and be responsible for the content and form of communication (Underberg, 2011). These areas apply to both written and oral communication, but the lines between them have been blurred substantially by technology. Is an online "chat" written or oral communication? Is texting more like talking or writing? The distinction is probably less important than the possibilities provided by technology to communicate clearly, responsibly, and fluently and be able to listen well.

At the University of North Carolina at Greensboro (2011), communication scholarship is described in terms of *voice*: public, changing, identity, and discovery. Researchers ask four questions that help define the role of communication: "How can communication scholarship . . ."

- Help us to understand and improve the quality of public discourse in the world around us?
- Help us engage with diversity, difference, and divisions in ways that promote understanding and collaborative/democratic change?
- Help us understand how people create and sustain desired identities and healthy relationships?
- Help us understand how people learn to co-construct, share, and critique knowledge?

These questions focus on the larger purposes of communication for individuals and a democratic society. They provide an important context for thinking about the use of technology in speaking and listening since the wiring of the world has intensified the public discourse across cultures, the potential for knowledge construction, and the way individuals create and share their identities.

Listening

Listening has long been tied to learning. Traditionally, students sitting in rows with folded hands and eyes front, listening intently to their teachers, were thought to be learning. This model does not reflect what we have learned about how students learn effectively. However, the importance of listening has not been diminished. Listening skills are essential for learning, enabling the acquisition of insights and information while enhancing interactions with others (Hunsaker, 1990). Recording and playback tools can help enhance learning by being a source of interesting oral presentations and opening the students' work up to a wider audience.

Listening is for both comprehending and for acquisition of information (Richards, 2008). Listening for *comprehension* offers a traditional way of thinking about the nature of listening where the purpose is to gain understanding. Listening for *acquisition* suggests that listeners can acquire information and additional proficiency from listening. In his work, Underwood (1990) suggests that teachers need to expose students to a range of listening experiences, make listening purposeful, help students understand the skills involved in listening, and help build student confidence in listening. The role of the teacher in helping students learn to listen has also been equated to a tailor finding the best fit for the students, a doctor diagnosing student needs, a detective continually asking whether the students will comprehend, an engineer who understands the workings of all the components, or a spy trying to figure out what the students are doing. We find that using analogies with students and having them create others makes them more active listeners. Post at least one of these analogies for each listening activity.

Even in informal, one-on-one, and small group communication, listening takes place at two levels. First, listening is a thoughtful act of *hearing* the words they are saying; breaking down the words, phrases, and sentences; and decoding them into their direct meaning. Second, listening is a process of *thinking* (Robert & Billings, 2009). The listener must make meaning from what she is hearing—analyzing the content and weighing it against prior experiences. Thus, each time a conversation occurs, the speaker and listener enter into a collaboration—sharing ideas, negotiating meaning, and developing a shared experience.

Learning to listen is fundamentally a metacognitive task. Learning to think about listening, students become aware of factors influencing their comprehension (Goh, 2002). The metacognitive listening process consists of three components: (1) identifying the *purpose* of the listening, (2) *self-monitoring* while listening, and (3) *self-evaluating*. Students must first set a purpose for their listening. Why are they listening? Knowing the purpose of their listening, students can be prepared to get the necessary content and context. Students who are self-monitoring their listening are continually checking their understanding, ensuring they are not missing important ideas or concepts. In evaluating their comprehension after listening, listeners are continually looking to improve their listening skills and maximize their learning (Goh, 2002).

Common Core State Standards

The Common Core State Standards for Speaking and Listening (www.corestandards.org) emphasize comprehension and collaboration, and the communication of knowledge and ideas. The following CCSS are identified throughout this section.

Key Ideas and Details

Grades K-5

- Quote accurately from a text when explaining what the text says explicitly and when drawing inferences from the text.

- Determine two or more main ideas of a text and explain how they are supported by key details; summarize the text.

- Explain the relationships or interactions between two or more individuals, events, ideas, or concepts in a historical, scientific, or technical text based on specific information in the text.

Grades 6–12

- Cite the textual evidence that most strongly supports an analysis of what the text says explicitly as well as inferences drawn from the text.

- Determine a theme or central idea of a text and analyze its development over the course of the text, including its relationship to the characters, setting, and plot; provide an objective summary of the text.

- Analyze how particular lines of dialogue or incidents in a story or drama propel the action, reveal aspects of a character, or provoke a decision.

Integration of Knowledge and Ideas

Grades K-5

- Draw on information from multiple print or digital sources, demonstrating the ability to locate an answer to a question quickly or to solve a problem efficiently.
- Integrate information from several texts on the same topic in order to write or speak about the subject knowledgeably.

Grades 6–12

- Analyze the extent to which a filmed or live production of a story or drama stays faithful to or departs from the text or script, evaluating the choices made by the director or actors.
- Analyze how a modern work of fiction draws on themes, patterns of events, or character types from myths, traditional stories, or religious works such as the Bible, including describing how the material is rendered anew.

Speaking and Listening

Grades K-5

- Engage effectively in a range of collaborative discussions (one-on-one, in groups, and teacher-led) with diverse partners on *grade 5 topics and texts*, building on others' ideas and expressing their own clearly.
- Summarize a written text read aloud or information presented in diverse media and formats, including visually, quantitatively, and orally.
- Summarize the points a speaker makes and explain how each claim is supported by reasons and evidence.
- Report on a topic or text or present an opinion, sequencing ideas logically and using appropriate facts and relevant, descriptive details to support main ideas or themes; speak clearly at an understandable pace.
- Include multimedia components (e.g., graphics, sound) and visual displays in presentations when appropriate to enhance the development of main ideas or themes.
- Adapt speech to a variety of contexts and tasks, using formal English when appropriate to task and situation.

Grades 6–12

- Engage effectively in a range of collaborative discussions (one-on-one, in groups, and teacher-led) with diverse partners on *grade 8 topics, texts, and issues,* building on others' ideas and expressing their own clearly.
- Analyze the purpose of information presented in diverse media and formats (e.g., visually, quantitatively, orally) and evaluate the motives (e.g., social, commercial, political) behind its presentation.

- Initiate and participate effectively in a range of collaborative discussions (one-on-one, in groups, and teacher-led) with diverse partners on *grades 11–12 topics, texts, and issues,* building on others' ideas and expressing their own clearly and persuasively.

- Integrate multiple sources of information presented in diverse formats and media (e.g., visually, quantitatively, orally) in order to make informed decisions and solve problems, evaluating the credibility and accuracy of each source and noting any discrepancies among the data.

- Evaluate a speaker's point of view, reasoning, and use of evidence and rhetoric, assessing the stance, premises, links among ideas, word choice, points of emphasis, and tone used.

- Present information, findings, and supporting evidence, conveying a clear and distinct perspective, such that listeners can follow the line of reasoning, alternative or opposing perspectives are addressed, and the organization, development, substance, and style are appropriate to purpose, audience, and a range of formal and informal tasks.

- Make strategic use of digital media (e.g., textual, graphical, audio, visual, and interactive elements) in presentations to enhance understanding of findings, reasoning, and evidence and to add interest.

- Adapt speech to a variety of contexts and tasks, demonstrating a command of formal English when indicated or appropriate.

For updated standards and more information, visit the Common Core State Standards Initiative (www.corestandards.org).

4 Technology Tools for Speaking

The key question for students is, "How do you say something meaningful in a powerful way that engages your audience?" whether in conversation or making a presentation. Even for intrapersonal communication—talking to yourself by reflecting, or keeping a diary—thinking about how to frame your thoughts for later listening enhances the experience.

Technology can be used to (1) enhance oral communication, (2) reflect on an oral communication, (3) integrate media, and (4) reach audiences. Technology changes communication, in some ways returning it to the oral traditions of the past:

> Humankind's oldest and newest thought-technologies are the oral tradition and the Internet. Despite superficial differences, both technologies are radically alike in depending not on static products but rather on continuous processes, not on 'What?' but on 'How do I get there?' In contrast to the fixed spatial organization of the page and book, the technologies of oral tradition and the Internet *mime the way we think* by processing along pathways within a network. In both media it's pathways—not things—that matter. (Pathways Project, 2011)

Now as in the past, communication is fundamentally about forming messages to convey meaning along pathways that others can navigate.

Unlike television and radio, current electronic communication offers massive amounts of raw data in many different forms that can be browsed, combed through, and reconfigured by the user (Rushkoff, 1999). As creators and providers of content for the web *and* as users of others' content, students can participate fully in the marketplace of ideas. The classroom provides an invaluable crucible for reflecting on and critiquing that participation so students develop the habit of being metacognitive about their communication.

The Center for Teaching and Learning at Stanford University suggests decentralizing the talk in the classroom, making "talking to each other" the focus, rather than talking to the teacher. In this way, the teacher shares the authority with students for who speaks when and to whom. This shift increases the amount of talk about learning among students and their time on task, while developing students' communication skills. The increased level of student talk about learning can lay the groundwork for using technology to record and share their voices.

In this chapter we discuss the various ways technology can be used to develop students' speaking skills in conversations, in small group discussions, and in prepared speeches. The best technology to use is often the one you have and understand how to use. The specific tools are changing all the time. We suggest the following tools and techniques as examples.

- Think Alouds—"notes to myself"
- Recording-Assisted Reading
- Partner Reading
- Call and Response
- Choral Reading
- Retelling
- Making Speeches

Think Alouds

In *reflecting*, students are practicing *intrapersonal* communication. Oral diaries, author notes, and study notes can all be created orally, recorded, and replayed. Cell phone apps provide an easy way to do this. Most 12–17-year-olds now own cell phones and most of these phones are "smart," containing all of the necessary technology for recording voice. A Pew Internet & American Life Project report in April 2010 found that 75% of teens owned cell phones, up from 45% in 2004, and teachers are finding educational uses for them that mirror workplace uses (Neilsen & Webb, 2011). For example, AudioBoo has a mobile platform app so students can use their own personal mobile device (iPhone, Android, Nokia with Blackberry, and Windows Mobile on the way) for recording, email the "boo," or simply phone it in. This app lets you see your sound levels as you are recording, add a picture, and then post it as a podcast or to a social networking site. It attaches a map and lets you search by location to hear other recordings from that geographical area. You can also follow people's recordings like you do on other social networking sites.

Using the Technology—AudioBoo

AudioBoo is web-based audio software that allows you to record and share audio with friends, family, your students, or the entire planet if you so desire. To get started, as with just about anything online these days, you must first create an account. It is very simple and only takes a few seconds. Pick a user name, enter your email, pick a password, and you are in. Figure 4.1 shows the AudioBoo account homepage I set up in about one minute . . .

A nice feature of AudioBoo is that you can have email messages automatically sent to you when a comment is posted to your "boo" or when others are following you. You can also be notified when you receive a message. Once you are all set up and have something to record, simply hit "Make a Recording/Upload File" and it opens a new control window. There is also a tutorial video that covers all the basics rather nicely and only takes a few minutes to watch. As you will see in the video, you and your students can create a social network by following each other and anyone else who may be talking about similar things that you are studying or exploring.

Figure 4.1 AudioBoo homepage

Consider adding Think Alouds to any field trip by having students record their reflections and take pictures along the way. You can leave it open-ended, just asking them to make some minimum number of recordings (five to six) that have to do with the purpose of the field trip, or you can give them a list of concepts to illustrate during the trip. For example, a trip to Sturbridge Colonial Village (in Massachusetts) could be differentiated by having some students describe at least five careers in the village with pictures of people engaged in that work, while others focus on the tools they used, the products they created, or the architecture of the buildings. When all the recordings are posted, they can be searched by location so each student will have contributed to understanding that part of the village with his or her recording and pictures.

You can take this idea up a level in a field study by having small groups of students record their observations or data over time in different locations. For example, for the study of a nearby forest ecosystem, teams of students could report about the plants, temperature, humidity, soil characteristics, light, animals, and topography weekly throughout the year. For geography, social studies, history, foreign language, and art teachers, there is another tool that links voice recordings to geographic locations. Woices (Woices.com) is a free web application, also available on most smartphones, that allows the user to upload a custom map or Google map, locate places of interest on the map, and then add media to accompany the identified locations. This emerging technology, co-locating space with speech, allows for rich storytelling and information sharing about the physical world of the students. Consider a history assignment that has the students locating the nearest historical landmark to their home, going there, and recording images and video while narrating the experience for the listener. The possibilities for these types of software are endless, and we find exploring their application across subjects very exciting.

Recording-Assisted Reading

Another oral reading technique is recording-assisted reading. In its original form, students listened to a book on tape read by a fluent reader and then read along with the tape to increase their own fluency.

We recommend having *your students create* the recordings of texts for other students or for students in younger grades. The users of the recordings could be the wider network of Internet users, a class of younger students in your school, or the students in your own classes who are recording significant passages for each other. For example, students can write poems, record their poetry (using AudioBoo or other tools), and share the recording with the whole class. A picture of the text of the poem can be posted with it. Listeners hear the poems and can respond with a recorded reaction (perhaps using VoiceThread). The whole class can also read along with recordings in choral reading style. To create a class study guide, students make recordings of significant passages from a common text that are then shared with the whole class. Ask students to comment on why they thought the passage was significant. The most significant passages will appear more than once in the collection. You can also ask provocative questions that students have to answer about passages of text, such as, "What was the author trying to accomplish by having the main character be so confused?"

CCSS Connection

- Engage effectively in a range of collaborative discussions (one-on-one, in groups, and teacher-led) with diverse partners building on others' ideas and expressing their own clearly.

For example, in a school that Brad used to work in, classes of older students were "buddied" with classes of younger students. They would meet once a month or more and spend time together. Often, the older students would read with their buddies. Recording themselves telling stories is a great way for the older students to master reading skills, further developing their technology literacy while offering something to the younger students in the school. Work with a buddy teacher or buddy class at your school or a nearby school to develop student relationships and use them to help students of both ages. The collection of read-alouds created by older students can become a listening center for the younger students that is accessible all the time, rather than just once a month when the older students come to visit.

Partner Reading

In partner reading, students take turns reading passages from a text. The technique engages the students with the text and each other, requiring them to alternate between reading and listening. Ask them to stop regularly to reflect on what they have read and to predict what will happen next. If you want them to work on fluency, have them record their readings and review them before talking about them. If the goal is predicting, have them record their predictions, then play them back after they have read further to discuss any unforeseen events, and revise their predictions in other areas.

Partners for partner reading can be chosen in a variety of ways. Consider pairing a strong reader with a weaker reader, allowing students to pick their own partner, pairing students randomly, or pairing them according to what they are reading. After students have been paired, they begin reading and writing in a partner journal. The partner journal can be one digital notebook to which they both contribute. They should first share reading duties, taking turns reading and discussing meaning while at the same time recording what they have discussed and learned in their journal. They should also take turns leading the reading discussion. Taking the activity further, student pairs can develop discussion questions based on their reading.

CCSS Connection

- Engage effectively in a range of collaborative discussions (one-on-one, in groups, and teacher-led) with diverse partners on *topics, texts, and issues,* building on others' ideas and expressing their own clearly.
- Initiate and participate effectively in a range of collaborative discussions (one-on-one, in groups, and teacher-led) with diverse partners on *topics, texts, and issues,* building on others' ideas and expressing their own clearly and persuasively.

Call and Response

Smitherman (1977) defines call and response as "spontaneous verbal and non-verbal interaction between speaker and listener in which all of the statements ('calls') are punctuated by expressions ('responses') from the listener" (p. 104). These interactions tend to be more repetitive than verbal duels and lack their argumentative form with their inherent goal of "winning." Instead, call and response feels more collaborative, and even like ritualized support. For example, in a study of call and response in classrooms, Foster (2011) describes a kind of salute beginning with the teacher's call, "What do we say?" followed by the students' response in unison, "You get down, baby!" In another example of call and response, whenever a student used more sophisticated vocabulary, he got to ring a bell, and then the class sang the chorus of *You Can Ring My Bell.* Having some class rituals can teach students the technique. For enhancing learning, students can research some examples of call and response in musical lyrics, then create their own, record them to refine them, and share them. Students can create their own call and response dialogues to capture the way people support other people, causes, and candidates.

Choral Reading

Choral reading is like reader's theater in that students have the texts in front of them, and different parts of the texts are assigned to individuals, small groups, or the whole group. The focus is on intonation and other voice qualities, as well as the coordination of the parts. Many examples of choral reading can be found on YouTube. A written example (Bean, 2011) follows. Notice how "characters" have been assigned to different parts of the text to provide guidance to those reading it.

The Preamble of the Constitution of the United States

Group 1:	*We*
All:	*The People*
Group 2:	*Of the United States*
Judge:	*In order to form*
Group 3:	*A more perfect union*
Judge:	*Establish justice*
Mother:	*Insure domestic tranquility*
Soldier:	*Provide for the common defense*
Group 1:	*Promote the general welfare*
Minister:	*And secure the blessings*
Soldier:	*Of liberty*
Group 2:	*To ourselves*
Mother:	*And our posterity*
Minister:	*Do ordain*
Judge:	*And establish*
Group 3:	*This constitution for*
All:	*The United States of America*

It's interesting to have several small groups of students create a choral reading script or performance for the same text. It shows students how many options there are for portraying ideas and where different emphases can be placed. As with the other oral techniques, getting a choral reading right takes practice, and recording the practice sessions and playing them back make students more conscious of what they are doing. The final version can be audio- or videotaped and shared with a wider audience.

Retelling

In *retelling*, students read or write about something and then retell it in their own words (Simcock, 1993). This requires them to process what they are reading, find their own words to communicate the meaning accurately to the listener, and adjust their retelling based on the listener's reaction. They have to think about what they need to communicate, how to do it differently than just reading it aloud, and, at the same time, how the listener is responding.

CCSS Connection

- Adapt speech to a variety of contexts and tasks, using formal English when appropriate to task and situation.

To enhance this activity with technology, have the student record his or her retelling and then play it for a listener. That way, they can be the observer during the listening and even interview the listener about what he or she heard to gauge the quality of the retelling. A variation of this is to have several students record retellings of the same text (fiction or nonfiction), and then other students compare the retellings. This makes the retellers want to do well since their retelling will be compared with others. It also has the advantage of the listeners hearing multiple retellings, which increases their comprehension. Retellings can be used with complex literacy texts, dense nonfiction passages, or descriptions of experiments or events. Use them whenever you know students will struggle with content to jumpstart deeper discussions. For example, after watching a presidential debate, students choose one issue to "retell" each candidate's position. They record their retellings using AudioBoo and then review each others' retellings (at least three), rating them on a scale from 1–3, with 1 = not accurate, 2 = mostly accurate, and 3 = completely accurate.

Speech Making

Good speeches take preparation, practice, and effective presentation. Web tools such as English Central (englishcentral.com) emphasize that "sound is social" and allow users to record and share audio with others. Feedback comes from others who listen, and most importantly from students listening to their own recordings and critiquing them so they internalize the criteria for effective communication. Discussions among students can focus on a question like, *How do I say something meaningful in a powerful way that engages my audience?* as they listen to their recordings. Not unlike a writer's group, the discussions can be frank since all the students are putting their work out there for critique.

CCSS Connection

Present information, findings, and supporting evidence, conveying a clear and distinct perspective, such that listeners can follow the line of reasoning, alternative or opposing perspectives are addressed, and the organization, development, substance, and style are appropriate to purpose, audience, and a range of formal and informal tasks.

An incredible resource for speeches is http://americanrhetoric.com. Containing Iraq war speeches to presidential presentations to the latest from the Secretary of State and from honorees at various events, this speech bank of videos is extensive and searchable. The text of the speeches is available so students can study the content as well as the delivery. Have students find multiple speeches on the same topic to compare how they are constructed, their purpose, and context. Students can identify styles they admire and try to deliver a speech by that person, while recording it so they can review it to see how they did.

While there is great benefit in students re-recording their own speeches as part of "practice makes perfect," they may also want to edit their final speeches and add music or other sound elements. Audacity (http://audacity.sourceforge.net/) and Aviary (www.aviary.com/) are free, open-source software programs for recording and editing sounds. Either application is very useful in recording and editing speech. Audacity is a program that you download to your computer. You use Aviary online.

Using the Technology—Aviary

To use Aviary, open your web browser and type in this link, http://advanced.aviary.com/launch/myna. It will take you directly to the audio editing and production software that is ready to use, as pictured in Figure 4.2.

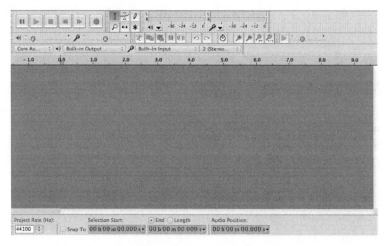

Figure 4.2 Aviary audio software

From here, you can begin to build your audio file. It allows for importing files, using developed audio files, editing, combining, recording, and more. Creating a file is fairly intuitive. Perhaps the best way to get to know the software is to play around with it. Have fun, drag and drop some of the pre-made files into the track bar, add additional tracks, record your voice, or import a favorite sound file. The best part is that you can't break it. Playing with technology does afford this wonderful opportunity to explore.

When you go to save your file, you will be prompted to log in or create an account. This is simple and free. Once you have created an account, it will save your audio file in your new account. It can be shared from there, edited again, or removed.

Summary

Using technology can enhance the process of learning to speak well. By recording their own voices, students can self-correct, becoming more aware of how they communicate. The recorded message or speech lets students hear themselves outside of their own heads so they automatically become more objective. By listening to other students' recordings, they learn from those who have skills slightly better than theirs. By getting feedback from teachers in audio commentaries, they are able to accept and use it more readily to improve.

5 Technology Tools for Listening

If speaking is silver, then listening is gold.

—Turkish Proverb

Around bedtime, a common occurrence in many a child's bedroom is a parent reading out loud a favorite story. Reading to children often continues only until they begin to read on their own, with the focus then shifting to getting them to read more and more. While reading skills are extremely important, the value of listening for the child should not be overlooked and may offer advantages in learning vocabulary and understanding meaning, even after they are reading on their own (Elley, 1989). This chapter provides examples of some technologies that we find offer unique and interesting ways of exposing students to listening for learning.

It may seem like a constant fight for students' attention. Are they listening to me? If they would only put their cell phones away and stop texting, we might make some progress. If you feel like this, you are certainly not alone. Listening is a skill—one that needs to be nurtured as you would any other skill and that only comes with practice, patience, and perseverance.

At its core is the motivation to learn, or simply to understand, so along with teaching students *how* to listen, it is necessary to engage them with what you are saying. Students can be engaged in effective communication in three ways: (1) in one-way communication in which the students are engaged as your audience through rhetorical questions, carefully constructed presentations, and multimedia; (2) in interactive communication in which the students are respondents, asking questions, adding ideas, and reacting to your presentation; and (3) in transactional communication in which the communication evolves based on the discussion of the topic by you *and* your students. In this chapter we discuss six strategies for using technology with listening:

- One-way communication to an audience
- Interactive communication between a speaker and respondents
- Listening to learn
- Assessment
- Active listening
- Listening to learn—podcasts, digital libraries
- Differentiating with sound (amplification, headsets)

One-Way Communication

In one-way communication, students are an audience listening to someone deliver a speech, soliloquy, tirade, lecture, stream of consciousness, or any other form of nonstop speech. The requirement of the listener is to be attentive (or at least look attentive, Hilarie liked to tell her students) and to attempt to understand the content. The beauty of listening to a speech rather than reading it is that the listener gets information from the intonation, emphasis, and pacing of the speaker. Good listeners prepare to listen *before* a speech; think *during* the speech, taking notes about the important ideas; and then review and organize their notes soon *after* the speech. They prepare to listen by making sure they understand the purpose of the lecture, downloading the slide show or other materials ahead of time, reading about the topic, and/or looking up information about the speaker. During the lecture, they think about what is being said so they are able to take notes about what is important and put it in the context of the larger picture; they also take notes about their own understanding as it develops during the speech. They may even jot down questions that come to mind that may be answered later in the speech or can be looked up afterward. After the speech, they review and edit their notes so they are organized around the topic, key ideas, or the relationships among the ideas. These notes represent the person's understanding of the content of the speech.

Technology can enhance all these elements of listening. When you or other speakers focus on what is required of the listener, it changes how you prepare, deliver, and follow up the speech. For example, you can post your slides or an outline ahead of time to be downloaded. Reading this material ahead of time frees the listener to think more and focus less on taking notes. It also gives the listener an accurate organizer that shows them the big ideas and the supporting details, examples, and references. During the speech, the listeners can add their own notes and questions right in the slide show, outline, or concept map. Afterward, they can email or post to a discussion their unanswered questions or points of confusion.

Even if the speaker is not focused on the listener's comprehension needs, technology can support *note-taking* and comprehension of the listener. By taking notes on the computer, the listener can jot down more information than when using paper and pencil, and in a flexible format. For example, concept mapping software allows the listener to put ideas in bubbles and then rearrange them, connect them, and take notes on them as his or her understanding develops. Even taking notes in a word processing document allows the listener to get more ideas down, rearrange them during the lecture, and refine them afterward. Embedding question marks in the notes lets the listener do a "find" for them later to search for answers. Taking notes electronically also makes it easy to share them with others for comparison, discussion, and improving understanding.

If speeches are *recorded*, they can be stopped and restarted and listened to more than once. This control allows the listeners to be totally focused on their understanding. As soon as they feel they are "lost" or missing something, they can stop and repeat the previous section, pause to reflect for a moment to get back on track, or review their prior notes or the outline of the speech. Significant passages can be listened to several times, while they review and add to the notes. For example, consider recording your introductory lecture to a genre, such as science fiction. Have students listen to the lecture outside of class and take notes in a diagram form. In class, have them compare their diagrams, discussing similarities and differences and revising their own diagram as necessary. Particularly interesting for this assignment is how students cope with understanding "science fiction." After reading some science fiction, ask students to revisit the lecture and their diagrams, adding examples.

Interactive Communication

In interactive communication, the listener is expected to respond, give feedback, and/or react to a communication. VoiceThread lets anyone create slides with audio (and video in the upgraded version). The platform is web based, and while it is not free, it offers a secure environment for a group to interact using voice, text, audio files, or video to discuss images, documents, and videos. A voice thread can be posted on the public site or only within the group. Once it is posted, other people can make comments—by adding their own voice threads. All the responses appear around the original slide show; hence, the individual reactions are seen by the group.

CCSS Connection

- Make strategic use of digital media (e.g., textual, graphical, audio, visual, and interactive elements) in presentations to enhance understanding of findings, reasoning, and evidence and to add interest.

- Adapt speech to a variety of contexts and tasks, demonstrating a command of formal English when indicated or appropriate.

Using the Technology—VoiceThread

VoiceThread is a collaborative multimedia slide show containing audio, video, and documents. To get started, go to VoiceThread.com and click on "Sign In or Register." Registration is free and only takes a few minutes with an email address. Once you have created an account, you will be taken to your new homepage, which will look something like our TechforLearning homepage shown in Figure 5.1.

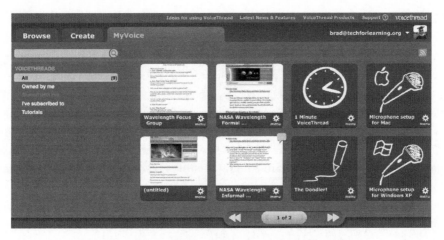

Figure 5.1 TechforLearning page on VoiceThread

Your account will be populated with a few voice threads right from the start. The first one, with the clock as the image, is a very easy to understand one-minute instructional video about getting started in VoiceThread. The others are also very helpful tutorials that will walk you through the different features VoiceThread offers and help you think about what your voice threads will look like. There is also an educators guide available as a .pdf that can be found following the link at the end of this box. You can print a few copies of the guide and let your students look through them before they get started and keep them with them while they work. Check out the educator's guide and download it for referring to in the future: http://voicethread.com/media/misc/getting_started_educator_mpb.pdf.

Why use an audio tool like VoiceThread? In a recent study conducted by Sue Sipple (Sipple and Sommers, 2005), college composition students reported a strong preference for **audio commentary**. They hypothesize that it provides the personal affective connection of a one-on-one conference and the more formal written feedback on papers. Lotus Perry of the University of Puget Sound describes how the audio tool Yackpack allows her to give students audio assignments to record once or twice a week (Perry, 2008). She listens to each one and gives the students audio feedback. She feels these assignments have improved their learning, because she can give them individualized specific feedback about their language development. She has noticed that they are eager for her feedback and that hearing her recorded critiques and encouragement on a regular basis has also created a positive relationship with her students. She notes that it has also made the students more supportive of each other since they can hear each other's recordings and her feedback. VoiceThread provides a similar environment for students to record assignments and then listen to teacher feedback and respond to the comments in a revised recording or in the next assignment. It is an excellent tool for nonfiction assignments. Have students post summaries of different passages. They will differ slightly, but the main ideas will come through.

Listening to Learn

Listening to speeches online can add to a student's understanding of a topic. The American Rhetoric website described in Chapter 4 is a wonderful resource for contemporary speeches that let students hear firsthand from thought leaders. YouTube is also a good resource for speeches from people from all different positions and roles in the world—from comedians to individuals, to politicians and professors. While iTunes is synonymous with music, it also has lots of free podcasts available for download. Students can practice note-taking when listening to podcasts on educational topics. Audible.com is a paid lending library of recorded books that may interest avid readers. One of our favorite podcasts is Radio Lab (radiolab.org). The topics range from politics to parasites, and the presentation style is conversational. We suggest students listen to a podcast twice, the first time to get the big ideas and a second time to fill in the details.

> ### *CCSS Connection*
>
> - Evaluate a speaker's point of view, reasoning, and use of evidence and rhetoric, assessing the stance, premises, links among ideas, word choice, points of emphasis, and tone used.

Assessment

Student assessment garners great attention from researchers, and it is increasingly important to be able to effectively assess student learning in a variety of ways associated with the many ways learning takes place. Continual and ongoing assessment allows teachers to monitor whether students have learned and the effectiveness of their own teaching. Quality assessment of students over time is clearly linked to student performance, and research consistently shows that monitoring and feedback are integral to student learning. What you assess and offer feedback on tells your students what you value and what is important.

Many technology tools exist that enable teachers to capture the verbal changes in their students over time. Lingt Classroom (formally Lingt—http://lingtlanguage.com) is primarily designed for foreign-language teachers, but we believe that it has numerous applications beyond foreign language-instruction. If you happen to be a foreign-language teacher, then you get a double benefit. Lingt provides web tools for language instruction in and outside of the classroom, including creating online assignments that are both engaging and easily assessed, making oral exams, offering targeted feedback for individual responses, incorporating video and images, and archiving all assignments and student work. Capturing, reviewing, and refining verbal output facilitates student assessment.

Active Listening

Active listeners consider multiple factors when interpreting a message, including the content, context, their own and the other person's experience and feelings, nonverbal cues such as facial expression and gestures, and qualities of the voice (pitch, loudness, rhythm, and speed). Students with good listening skills are generally more successful learners than are their peers who don't listen. They tend to understand and follow directions the first time. They actively connect what they know with what they are hearing so they build their knowledge. Active listening also aids with concentration and memory. Active listeners tend to get more help and interest from speakers, since they feel they have an attentive audience (Learning Through Listening, 2011). Choose or have students choose a video recording of a speech that they will then view five times, watching for a different one of the following areas each time:

1. Content—What do they say? What words do they use?
2. Context—Who is the intended audience? Why is this person speaking on this topic? What is the physical setting?

3. Feelings—What emotion does the speaker express? What feelings is he or she trying to evoke in the listener? What emotional reaction does the student have?

4. Nonverbal information—For this analysis, students should turn off the sound so they can focus on the nonverbal communication, including facial expressions and gestures.

5. Voice characteristics—For this analysis, students should sit where they can hear, but not see the video, or turn the screen to black to make notes about the pitch, loudness, rhythm, and speed of the speaker's voice.

After analyzing the video from the five different perspectives, students will be able to describe in depth how the speaker got his or her point across in terms of the five areas and to make recommendations for strengthening the communication in each area.

We like to have students analyze speeches online, then record their own, and critique each others' speeches. If you have students do this throughout the year for different kinds of speeches (persuasive, informative, interview) they will end up with a portfolio of work that will show their skill development. If you keep the first version and final version of each speech, it shows growth very clearly.

Differentiating with Sound (Amplification, Headsets)

Sometimes students don't listen because they can't hear, either because of noise, echo, distance from the speaker, or a hearing impairment. Using a "sound field amplification system," the teacher wears a wireless headset that transmits his or her voice to a speaker that enhances its volume. When set up and maintained properly, this system provides consistent high-quality sound from the teacher's voice so all students can hear and listen better.

Several organizations provide audio recordings of texts to support students with visual impairments or learning disabilities that make reading difficult. Learning Ally (www.learningally.org) was founded in 1948 as Recording for the Blind. They serve more than 300,000 K–12, college, and graduate students; veterans; and lifelong learners. On their website, they state, "Learning Ally's collection of more than 65,000 digitally recorded textbooks and literature titles—downloadable and accessible on mainstream as well as specialized assistive technology devices—is the largest of its kind in the world." The Recorded Books site (http://recordedbooks.com), now merged with Simply Books, offer titles for rent or purchase to individuals and libraries. Talking Books is a free library service available to U.S. residents and citizens living abroad whose low vision, blindness, or physical handicap makes it difficult for them to read a standard printed page. Local cooperating libraries throughout the United States mail National Library Service audiobooks, magazines, and audio equipment directly to enrollees at no cost (www.nlstalkingbooks.org).

Summary

Listening to stories is a fond memory for many of us, and with technology students have the opportunity to listen to many different kinds of recordings from people far and near. With technology, the listener can control the pace, volume, and repetitions. They can listen to something multiple times, in a location of their choice, and take notes at the same time. They can share recordings with others, add their own comments, and read others' comments. They can create recordings for others and gauge the effect on their listeners from their comments and questions.

6 | Using Technology for Speaking and Listening

These techniques use technology to enable students to practice speaking and listening in different formats. The basic strategy for using technology has three components: (1) recording students' initial ideas, (2) practice sessions, and (3) final presentations so they can self-correct and learn from each other. If you set time limits, you or the student can record voices on a phone and upload them easily. In this chapter we present five strategies for using technology for speaking and listening:

- Reader's Theater
- Verbal Dueling
- A New Take on Pen Pals
- Study Guides
- Improvisation and Role Playing

CCSS Connection

- Adapt speech to a variety of contexts and tasks, using formal English when appropriate to task and situation.
- Engage effectively in a range of collaborative discussions (one-on-one, in groups, and teacher-led) with diverse partners on *topics, texts, and issues*, building on others' ideas and expressing their own clearly.

Reader's Theater

In Reader's Theater, students read aloud from scripts. The emphasis is on oral expression and fluency. Unlike in regular theater productions, students do not memorize lines; there are no props, costumes, or sets. Like regular theater, students practice their lines, reading and rereading them, and in doing so increase their fluency. The story line, interaction, and discussion all aid with comprehension. This "guided repeated oral reading" has been found to have a significant and positive impact on word recognition, fluency, and comprehension across a range of grade levels (National Reading Panel, 1999). Search for "reader's theater" online and you will find sources for scripts and tips for how to use this strategy in your classroom: www.teachingheart.net/ readerstheater.htm, www.timelessteacherstuff.com, or www.readingonline.org/electronic/elec_ index.asp?HREF=carrick/index.html.

Use technology to enhance this technique by recording segments of the play for review by the cast. While it is helpful to discuss each student's rendition of his or her lines, it is even more helpful to have them be able to hear a recording of them. When they listen to a recording of their performance, they become part of the audience and so are able to better critique what they did. Encourage students to listen to the recording afterward and note the best moments, what they would improve on, and what they learned about speaking from the exercise.

A recording of the final performance can also be "broadcast," preferably in acts, on the Internet to increase the audience and make the performance accessible to friends and family who can make comments as listeners. As with a radio play, broadcasting makes it even clearer that the oral expression is "the thing." Having an audience outside the classroom increases students' motivation to product the best version they possibly can.

Verbal Dueling

For older students, consider verbal duels, a form of debate that is based on dialogue. Verbal duels are defined as "a genre of argumentative language that entails exchanges between two persons, parties, or characters that challenge each other to a performative display of verbal skillfulness in front of an audience" (Pagliai, 2009, p. 63). These duels can be spoken or sung, such as the "contrasto" performed by poets of central Italy, or rappers "battling" back and forth. The structure of a verbal duel is not unlike a debate in that the opposing sides state their positions, build a case through giving evidence for their position, and then have closing remarks that summarize their points and refute their opponent's points. In between the statements of evidence are rebuttals by the other side, and the format controls the time to give each side equal time.

CCSS Connection

- Evaluate a speaker's point of view, reasoning, and use of evidence and rhetoric, assessing the stance, premises, links among ideas, word choice, points of emphasis, and tone used.
- Present information, findings, and supporting evidence, conveying a clear and distinct perspective, such that listeners can follow the line of reasoning, alternative or opposing perspectives are addressed, and the organization, development, substance, and style are appropriate to purpose, audience, and a range of formal and informal tasks.

Unlike a debate, a verbal duel is much faster, with shorter presentations by each side; points are delivered with emotion and rebuttals can border on insults. Verbal prowess wins the duel. The back-and-forth format borders on performance art. Opponents develop their points and can set them in rhyme. Audio recording speeds up the effect of practice because the author gets immediate feedback by listening to the recording and can modify the presentation then. A recording of the actual duel allows you to stop it for segment-by-segment discussion in class after it is presented live. Conflicts within and between characters are especially well suited for this type of discussion, such as Hamlet's monologues about his internal struggles, the showdown between Beowulf and Unferth upon Beowulf's arrival at Heorot, Lincoln versus Jefferson Davis on slavery, or Churchill versus Hitler on sovereignty.

Before embarking on a verbal debate or duel on critical subjects, it may be beneficial to engage students in a few "practice" rounds so that they get the hang of things. One idea is to have students choose one of two sides in a debate and then have them be responsible for arguing the opposite side of the issue from what they chose. Give students very limited time to prepare and encourage them to work together to present a cohesive argument.

A New Take on Pen Pals

Consider connecting your students with other students as "pen pals" using a tool like Skype with voice over the Internet. Students can communicate one on one through school computers or on their personal computers outside of school, or mobile to mobile, depending on your school's policies. Skype-to-Skype calls are free; Skype calls to mobile or landline phones carry a charge. Students can interview each other about their local areas, current events, interests, and topics they are studying. Students need to communicate clearly and listen carefully to carry on a conversation and keep it interesting. Have students reflect on what makes a good speaker and a good listener in a conversation and then practice that in their conversations.

Using the Technology—Skype

We use Skype like we used to use the house phone. In fact, after nearly 50 years with two families and the same phone number for the house, we had the traditional "landline phone" shut off and have not missed it for a second.

To get started using Skype, visit the homepage (Skype.com) to get an account and download the software (it does need to be downloaded to your computer). Once on the homepage, choose "Join Skype" in the upper right and follow the prompts to create your account. After it has been created, you will be asked if you want to add credit to your account. Skype credit lets you call any number in the world just like you would using a traditional phone, but costs a lot less. When we add $20 to our account, it could last a year or more. However, you do not have to add credit to your account to use Skype. Quite the opposite—one of the many great things about using Skype is that it is free. You can Skype (using it as a verb here—you may also hear people say that they were "Skyping" with a friend) with anyone in the world who has a Skype account and it will cost you absolutely nothing!

With your new Skype account, you will want to add contacts, just like you would in your mobile phone or address book. It works mostly the same way. You simply click on "Add Contact" and search for the person you want to add. It is necessary to get their Skype

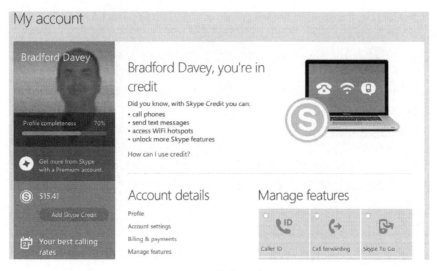

Figure 6.1 Personal Skype home page

name/contact information to contact them. Our Skype account homepage is shown in Figure 6.1.

Skype also has a bunch of other terrific features. As mentioned earlier, you can call any telephone number. You can also make group calls, send messages, video Skype, group video Skype, Skype to a mobile number, and have calls forwarded to another number. For educational purposes, Skype can allow you and your class to reach out and connect with people all over the world. We have heard of language classes using Skype to talk with people in different countries, science classes using it to talk with research scientists around the world, and teachers using it as a homework help line.

Study Guides

Students like to talk, often too much during class time. However, this is a tendency that can be used to help them learn. Consider utilizing a tool that allows students to share verbal information with each other. A tool like Voxopop (www.voxopop.com/) enables students and teachers to form talk groups that are engaging and easy to for the students to use. Voxopop "talkgroups" (as they are called) are like discussion boards or message boards, but use voice in place of traditional text. The talkgroups are available any time and any place, enabling students with varying schedules to participate when and how they can, adding flexibility to student learning.

For study guides, set up the discussion with the key topics and then ask students to record important ideas for each topic as they read and study. All the recordings will be archived and grouped by topic for all the students to review. To differentiate instruction, designate some of the quick thinkers as editors with the task of rearranging or adding synthesizing comments. You can build up to organizing the discussion around essential questions. Ask students to respond with a voice recording of their response to each question, a reading of an important passage, or an important reference. Encourage them to be "thought" leaders in their recordings, reporting for an audience interested in learning about the idea but struggling with the essential question.

Improvisation and Role Playing

Improvisation activities are based on elements that the "actors" put together into a performance. Actors can be handed a series of unrelated quotations from prominent figures or movies, given a situation, or handed a prop. They then work to weave these elements together to make sense. The listening audience is generally amused, and often informed, by how the actors put the disparate elements together. Encourage students to use technology like phones and sound effects in their performances. Set a time limit of five to eight minutes, record, and post them so students can view and comment on them. There are several examples of improvisation activities. Students can be the characters from a play or story, but then have to use movie lines in talking about an event from the text, citing the dialogue as best they can. Or, given a historical situation, actors have to interview a set of "people on the street" while discussing the situation. For more improv ideas and examples, check out the pages of professional improv companies (http://fuzzyco.com/improv/).

CCSS Connection

- Adapt speech to a variety of contexts and tasks, demonstrating a command of formal English when indicated or appropriate.

The benefits of role playing are increased student interest in the subject matter (Poorman, 2002), increased involvement in learning (Fogg, 2011), and building empathy in students by having them experience a different perspective (McGregor, 1993; Poorman, 2002). You can give students monologues or dialogues to read or have them create their own based on research on the character. Listeners can describe the characters based on how the "actors" portrayed them. Consider having different students do the same character so listeners have multiple portrayals. This works especially well with historical figures and characters. It's also fun (and effective) to put the character in a new setting, like a different time period, or in conversation with someone they didn't or couldn't have known about on a topic of common interest. What if Newton and Einstein could have a conversation? Or Obama and his father? Or Eleanor Roosevelt and Hilary Clinton? Be sure to record and post these role plays, and encourage comments by teaching students how to offer constructive comments.

Conclusions

Speaking and listening activities give a major boost to reading and writing development. They are fun, natural, and usually interactive, so students are more engaged and motivated to do their best. The social aspect of speaking and listening immediately makes students more self-aware and interested in being successful. Technology contributes significantly by letting students listen to themselves. It gives them a chance to self-correct to meet their own standards and in areas where they can see others doing better. Speaking and listening connect students in the learning process so they are more likely to support each other in learning. Capturing audio exchanges using technology, and archiving them, exposes students to multiple perspectives, levels of skill, and models—all within their own class. Technology also allows students to dramatically increase their access to speeches, talks, lectures, and performances of others; to resources to create their own recordings; and to a larger audience on the Internet if they choose to post their recordings.

Key Ideas

- Speaking and listening are how we communicate first and most often even after we learn to read and write.

- Speaking allows some students to present their ideas more completely and fluently than writing.

- Audio recording of speech allows the listener to hear all of the aspects of speech and the speaker to capture it for themselves to review and improve on.

- Audio-captured speeches or conversations can become the basis for reading and writing.

- Speaking and listening are a medium for critical thinking.

- Technology tools for speaking and listening support individual differences in learning by offering multiple methods of presentation, expression and engagement.

- Listening to lyrics can involve students in understanding characters, themes, and cultures.

- Listening to recorded stories or texts engages some students better than reading.

- Listening to others gives students an opportunity to connect, engage, and collaborate.

- Creating recordings for sharing with a wider audience can encourage students to refine their ideas and expression.

References for Section II

Adler, M. (1983). *How to speak, how to listen*. Ann Arbor, MI: Macmillan.

Bean, L. (2011). *Choral reading*. Retrieved September 2011 from http://education.byu.edu/arts/documents/LisaBeanChoralReading.pdf.

Elley, W. (1989). Vocabulary acquisition from listening to stories. *Reading Research Quarterly, 24*(2), 174–187.

Fogg, P. (2001). A history professor engages students by giving them a role in the action. *Chronicle of Higher Education, 48*(12), A12–13.

Foster, M. (2001). Using call-and-response to facilitate language mastery and literacy acquisition among African American students. Retrieved online from www.cal.org/resources/digest/0204foster.html

Goh, C.C.M. (2002). *Teaching listening in the language classroom*. Singapore: Relc Portfolio Series 4.

Hohstadt, T., & Kast, D. (2009). The age of virtual reality. *American Communication Journal, 11*(1), 113–147.

Hunsaker, R. A. (1990). *Understanding and developing the skills of oral communication: Speaking and listening* (2nd ed.). New York: HarperCollins.

Learning Through Listening. (2011). *Learning ally*. Retrieved from www.learningthroughlistening. org/Listening-A-Powerful-Skill/Listening-and-Learning/Benefits-of-Teaching-Listening/93/.

McGregor, Joy. 1993. Cognitive processes and the use of information. *School Library Media Annual, 12*, 124–133.

McLuhan, M., with Fiore, Q. (1967). *The medium is the message*. New York: Random House.

Mehrabian, A. (1971). *Silent messages*. Oxford: Wadsworth.

National Reading Panel. (1999). *Report of the national reading panel: Teaching children to read—a summary report*. National Institute of Child Health and Human Development. Retrieved from www.cdl.org/resource-library/articles/report_nrp.php.

Neilsen, L., & Webb, W. (2011). *Teaching generation text: Using cell phones to enhance learning*. San Francisco: Jossey-Bass.

Pagliai, V. (2009). The art of dueling with words: Toward a new understanding of verbal duels across the world. *Oral Tradition, 24*(1), 61–88.

Pathways Project. (2011). *Welcome to the Pathways Project*. Retrieved from www.pathwaysproject. org/pathways/show/HomePage.

Perry, B. (2011). Creating an emotionally safe classroom. *Early Childhood Today*. Retrieved October 2011 from www.scholastic.com/teachers/article/emotional-development-creating-emotion ally-safe-classroom.

Perry, L. (2008, June 6). Teaching with the audio tool YackPack. *University of Puget Sound*. Retrieved from www.youtube.com/watch?v=OZ3IapmFhIQ.

Poorman, P.B. (2002). Biography and role-playing: Fostering empathy in abnormal psychology. *Teaching of Psychology, 29*(1), 32–36.

Richards, J. C. (2008). *Teaching listening and speaking: From theory to practice*. New York: Cambridge University Press.

Robert, T., & Billings, L. (2009). Speak and listen. *Kappan, 91*(2), 81–85.

Robert, T. and Billings, L. (2009). Speak up and listen. *National Paideia Center*. Obtained from http://files.eric.ed.gov/fulltext/ED513482.pdf.

Rushkoff, D. (1999). *Coercion: Why we listen to what "they" say*. New York: Riverhead Trade.

Schwartzman, R. (2010). Fundamentals of communication. In *Fundamentals of oral communication* (pp. 27–44). Dubuque, IA: Kendall Hunt.

Seeley-Case, T. (2010, Fall). *Fundamentals of oral communication course description*. College of Southern Ohio.

Simcock, M. (1993). Developing productive vocabulary using the "ask and answer" technique. *Guidelines, 15*(2), 1–7.

Sipple, S., & Sommers J. (2005). *A heterotopic space: Digitized audio commentary & student revisions*. Retrieved from www.users.muohio.edu/sommerjd.

Smitherman, G. (1977). *Talkin and testifyin: The language of Black America*. Detroit, MI: Wayne State University Press.

Underberg, L. (2011). *Fundamentals of oral communication course description*. Southeast Missouri State University.

Underwood, M. (1990). *Teaching listening*. Longman Handbooks for Language Teachers. London: Longman.

University of North Carolina at Greensboro. (2011). *Current research projects of the communication studies faculty*. Retrieved Dec. 1, 2011, from www.uncg.edu/cst/faculty/research.html.

Wallace, T., Stariha, W. E., & Walbert, H. J. (2004). *Teaching speaking, listening, and writing*. New York: UNESCO.

Viewing and Producing

Without image, thinking is impossible.

—Aristotle (1941, p. 607)

In this section we take a close look at viewing and producing. Like reading and writing, and listening and speaking, they are reciprocal processes. First, we provide some background on viewing and producing. In Chapter 7, we focus on strategies to develop students' critical viewing skills to enhance understanding. The focus of Chapter 8 is on activities that make students the producers of visual material that they develop from their own lives, school life, or backgrounds. In Chapter 9, we suggest ways you can have students view visual material to learn and as models to produce their own directions, guides, and multimodal presentations.

Key ideas

- Today's learners are immersed in a very visually stimulating media world.

- Images are highly engaging and convey large amounts of information, perhaps providing the experience closest to daily life.

- Children between the ages of 8 and 18 are exposed to an average of 10 hours of media daily (TV, music, computers, and video games); it is estimated that over 60% have a TV in their bedroom.

- Visual literacy standards have evolved to help teachers direct student learning and have been adopted by 49 states.

- Proficiency in 21st-century visual literacy includes developing skills with the tools of technology, designing and sharing information, managing, analyzing, and synthesizing multiple streams of simultaneous information and creating, critiquing, analyzing, and evaluating multimedia tasks.

- Proficiency in visual literacy also includes understanding how and why media messages are constructed, examining how individuals interpret messages differently, and understanding how media can influence beliefs and behaviors.

- Producing visual material is a natural continuation of mastering understanding of visual imagery.

Research on Technology for Viewing and Producing

Viewing

The utilization of visual images to communicate ideas has been part of human culture since before words were available. The relationship between verbal and visual information dates back thousands of years (Benson, 1997). In the same way our ancestors used environmental clues, we understand and communicate through *visual materials* (illustrations, diagrams, maps, and pictures). These visual images can be divided into the basic elements of the dot, line, shape, direction, tone, color, texture, dimension, scale, and movement (Dondis, 1973). Combined, these elements comprise one of the most profound and powerful developments since the printed word. The primary form of literacy of the 21st century has become visual (Frey & Fisher, 2008). The emergence of the "Net Generation" (Tapscott, 1997) has paralleled this change in literacy of the 21st century. Today's digitally savvy learners live in a media-immersive environment in which visual materials are essential. As in other areas of literacy, students need help in understanding, dissecting, and using visual material for communication. They may be visually oriented without being aware of the tools, strategies, and technologies that make them critical consumers of images.

Jones-Kavaller and Flannigan's (2006) research on media literacy suggests a lack of education in schools for 21st-century literacy skills. They suggest that "digitally literate students [are] being led by linear-thinking, technologically stymied instructors" (p. 8) who do not adequately integrate technology into learning objectives and lesson plans. The technology divide between tech-savvy students and their school experience continues to increase. Metros and Woolsey (2006) offer three ways to help students develop visual literacy and increase the relevance of school education: (1) teach the basic language of design; (2) provide opportunities and resources for learners to become visual producers; and (3) help develop visually literate learners able to judge the accuracy, validity, and worth of what they are experiencing.

Metros and Woolsey's (2006) visual literacy adoption ideas align with the rapid emergence of communication technologies now widely available online. Linguistic and non-linguistic types of information are commonly presented to the viewer in blended form in textbooks, webpages, Internet navigation bars, print and television advertisements, and instructional manuals (Benson, 1997). Learners are immersed in a blended media world and so have become familiar with the juxtaposition of text and other media. In educational settings, this juxtaposition enhances learning (Stokes, 2001): "Using visuals in teaching results in a greater degree of learning" (p. 1).

Perhaps it is the emergence of visual literacy standards themselves that mark the widespread recognition of the importance of helping students engage in active learning to understand, draw from, manipulate, and create with visual communication technologies. As of 2011, 49 of the 50 states have adopted technology and literacy standards. In all of these standards, "producing" takes a prominent role in the development of student literacy, in which students are developing their own understanding of literacy through direct interaction and manipulation of their own work and learning.

Producing

Audiovisual media offer students the opportunity to communicate their ideas in presentational forms rather than putting verbal and written models at the center (logocentric) of their learning and communication (Niesyto, Buckingham, & Fisherkeller, 2003). Increasingly, the global media system of pushed messages is being bucked by personal media production on the Internet where everyone can produce his or her own message, acting as entertainer, social messenger, self-promoter, or observer. Failing to recognize media as the predominant language of today's youth and incorporating it into the work of our schools may deepen the profound disconnect between students' social and cultural lives and school. Students producing their own media do not simply mimic or imitate. Instead, they play with different aspects of familiar themes and issues, transforming the experience of production to create unique messages in the forms they are used to consuming (Grace & Tobin, 2002).

Grace and Tobin (2002) further note that the videos the students produce are both similar to stories they might have written in a Language Arts assignment and yet different in how they combine a dynamic collaborative process with a sense of freedom to explore new ideas and interpretations. The combination of extralinguistic elements, body language, special effects, and performance raises the level of the written word to new heights. Technology tools now allow this to happen seamlessly in the classroom.

There are a variety of instructional techniques for the effective integration of digital media production at the student level, including the use of digital video projects in the classroom (Buckingham & Harvey, 2001; de Block & Rydin, 2006). Digital video production has been studied as a way of helping students in storytelling and narrative construction (Beilke & Stuve, 2004; Hull & Nelson, 2005) and has been effective in enabling new and dynamic outcomes in literacy and learning. The incorporation of video production makes multimedia approaches possible, transforming the classroom into a modern, fast-paced, media-rich, and familiar environment for the students to learn through doing.

Common Core State Standards for Viewing and Producing

What are the standards for viewing and producing? Each state has adopted its own variation of visual literacy standards. In 2002, South Carolina approved revised curriculum standards that included, for the first time, "viewing." In the South Carolina curriculum, viewing joins listening, speaking, reading, writing, and research as another important focus in the classroom; this inclusion of viewing recognizes the powerful force of visual media in the 21st century. The viewing strand refers to nonprint texts, which are defined as sources of information, such as television, radio, films, movies, videotapes, live performances, the Internet, and other multimedia technologies. One challenge is to help students make sense of all the media they encounter on a daily basis and respond to it personally, critically, and creatively. Students are exposed to and, for the most part, are conversant in the world of movies, television, video, video games, the Internet, and other emerging technologies (Baker, 2012), but need to become critical consumers and producers in these media. The Georgia state English and Language Arts standards include viewing as well:

> The English Language Arts Curriculum is designed to introduce students to core concepts that are further developed and expanded as students progress through each grade level. This process allows students to develop the skills necessary to: 1) comprehend and interpret texts, including written as well as audio and visual texts; 2) compose a variety of types of texts, including those critical to the workplace; 3) effectively communicate and interact with others in group situations; and 4) communicate information through different modes of presentation. The English Language Arts curriculum integrates the processes of reading, writing, and listening/speaking/viewing in order to help students communicate and interpret information in a variety of modes. (Georgia Department of Education)

This standard's explicit inclusion of visual texts and the communication of information through different modes of presentations illustrates the importance of viewing and producing. Most other states have similar standards. For example, the 2012 California Board of Education standard expects students to be able to interpret and evaluate the various ways that visual image makers (e.g., graphic artists, documentary filmmakers, illustrators, news photographers) present events and communicate information.

Common Core State Standards

Integration of Knowledge and Ideas

The Common Core Standards are identified throughout this section.
Grades K–5

- Analyze how visual and multimedia elements contribute to the meaning, tone, or beauty of a text (e.g., graphic novel, multimedia presentation of fiction, folktale, myth, poem).

- Draw on information from multiple print or digital sources, demonstrating the ability to locate an answer to a question quickly or to solve a problem efficiently.

- Integrate information from several texts on the same topic in order to write or speak about the subject knowledgeably.

Grades 6–12

- Analyze the extent to which a filmed or live production of a story or drama stays faithful to or departs from the text or script, evaluating the choices made by the director or actors.

- Analyze multiple interpretations of a story, drama, or poem (e.g., recorded or live production of a play or recorded novel or poetry), evaluating how each version interprets the source text. (Include at least one play by Shakespeare and one play by an American dramatist.)

- Evaluate the advantages and disadvantages of using different mediums (e.g., print or digital text, video, multimedia) to present a particular topic or idea.

- Integrate and evaluate multiple sources of information presented in different media or formats (e.g., visually, quantitatively) as well as in words in order to address a question or solve a problem.

- Use technology, including the Internet, to produce and publish writing and to interact and collaborate with others.

- Draw evidence from literary or informational texts to support analysis, reflection, and research.

Research to Build and Present Knowledge

Grades 6–12

- Gather relevant information from multiple print and digital sources, using search terms effectively; assess the credibility and accuracy of each source; and quote or paraphrase the data and conclusions of others while avoiding plagiarism and following a standard format for citation.

- Produce clear and coherent writing in which the development, organization, and style are appropriate to task, purpose, and audience.

For updated standards and more information, visit the Common Core State Standards Initiative (www.corestandards.org).

7 Technology Tools for Viewing

There are endless things to view on the Internet. That's the trouble: There are endless things to view on the Internet. Where does a teacher or student start? What tools and techniques are available that truly enhance learning while utilizing technology tools for viewing? For the purpose of learning, much of what is available online is one-way delivery material designed to offer information to the viewer. When viewing for information, the quality of the images and accompanying text or sound has increased a great deal over the years, and material is widely available. The most rapidly growing segment of viewed material on the Internet is video (Nielsen, 2009), with young adults in the 18–24 age group watching 5½ hours of video and movies online each day. This is more than social sites, games, and music combined. However, as students are introduced to social media younger and younger, this is changing.

In this chapter we discuss the implications of using a few particular technologies in an educational setting while looking more broadly at the educational pedagogy behind their use. The best technology to use is often the one you have and understand how to use. The specific tools are changing all the time. In this chapter, we present six strategies for using technology to enhance student viewing skills:

- Making Thinking Visible
- QR Codes
- Social Learning
- Viewing for Understanding
- Critical Viewing
- E-Readers

Making Thinking Visible

Often, while students may come to a correct answer or a reasonable solution, it is often difficult for them to explain how they got there or to show their thinking as they work to resolve the problem or answer the question. Making their thinking visible is one way of helping to bridge the gap between what goes on inside students' minds and what they write on paper. Concept mapping is one way of making thinking visible. It is also a good way for students to collaborate to develop an understanding of the relationship between different topics being covered and to ensure that all of the necessary areas are included. One such online concept mapping software is Gliffy (gliffy. com). With your school's nonprofit license, you can get their "confluence plugin" that will allow multiple users to work on maps together.

CCSS Connection

- Use technology, including the Internet, to produce and publish writing and to interact and collaborate with others.
- Draw evidence from literary or informational texts to support analysis, reflection, and research.

Using the Technology—Gliffy

To use Gliffy, like just about everything else online these days, you will need to create an account. It is free and takes only a few minutes. Once you have created your account, you log in each time you go to make a Gliffy. The first page you will see once you log in will be what you see in Figure 7.1.

Figure 7.1 Gliffy homepage

For this example, we are going to create a new document. So, we have clicked on "Create Document" under "A New Document." Once you do that, you will get to the page shown in Figure 7.2.

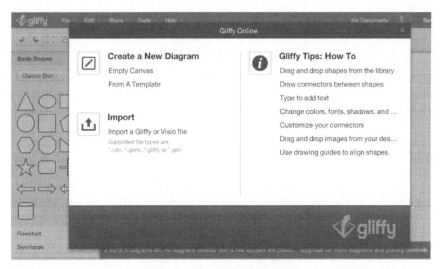

Figure 7.2 Gliffy prompt page

Once you choose the Gliffy template you want, choose "Create Document" at the bottom right and you are all done. Here we have chosen a blank page to work from (Figure 7.3).

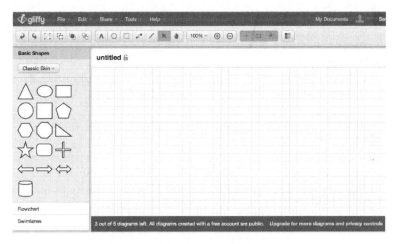

Figure 7.3 Gliffy creation page

The working interface in Gliffy is like that in most other mapping software and is fairly intuitive. Gliffy has a number of features that make its use easier. There are also some terrific examples of what people have created on the Gliffy website, which are worth looking at for ideas and inspiration.

Often, video available to view online is not suitable for all audiences because it is not closed captioned. The site 22 Frames (22Frames.com) captures and aggregates captioned videos from all over the world. Closed captioning is both a powerful tool for students with disabilities and a challenge for students developing their own videos to consider during production. It also makes more complex material accessible to students. While 22 Frames does have a number of videos available, they are limited in number and not every subject is covered. However, if you have students who need this type of resource, it is good to know closed captioning is out there and is growing daily. For many years, United Streaming offered free video content covering nearly every subject imaginable. Discovery Education (www.discoveryeducation.com/) acquired United Streaming a few years ago. In doing so, they made available its thousands of excellent quality videos—but at a cost. Their website does offer a collection of free materials as well, and so it is still worth a visit even if you do not subscribe.

QR Codes

Quick Response (QR) codes are beginning to show up all over the place (see Figure 7.4). We see them in magazines, newspapers, websites, business cards, books, and even on the sides of buildings. What really got our attention was seeing them in a textbook. The QR codes in the textbook linked to multimedia associated with the content being discussed or to webpages with additional readings. This was an interesting addition to the book. It did rely on students having smartphones that were able to scan a QR code and had an Internet connection (data package) to take them to the information. QR code readers are available on most smartphones and using most laptop webcams.

Consider developing a lesson plan using QR codes that will engage students in an interactive learning session. Instead of writing webpage links, you can give students a QR code to scan that takes them to some valuable resources. The QR codes should take them to something useful that makes the lesson more interesting and engaging. Links to images, videos, or voice recordings then help to promote discussion among the students. Students who are blogging or producing online can provide you with a QR code of their own that will take you and their classmates to their work.

On a recent visit to Philadelphia we found QR codes in historical buildings. What a great way to engage students! Better yet, have them create the QR codes themselves as a follow-up to a field trip. The research they do on the trip then gets put into resources others can use. They could also create QR codes for trees and plants on a nature trail, an orientation to the school for incoming students, or additional information for open houses.

Figure 7.4 QR code

Social Learning

By far, the biggest player in the online video world has to be YouTube. At the end of 2012, on YouTube over a half-million videos were viewed 3 billion times each day (www.youtube.com/t/press_statistics). While there are many (some would say most) videos on YouTube that have little or no educational value, there are some wonderful channels like NASA, NOAA, MIT, UCTelevision, FORAtv, and the Research Channel. On the NASA channel, students have access to NASA scientists and engineers from around the country passionately telling the world about their research. This passion is important for students to see, particularly from those in the STEM fields. YouTube offers educational videos at youtube.com/teachers. YouTube Teachers was created to help teachers introduce educational videos to students to educate, engage, and inspire. All of the videos available here are aligned with the Common State Standards. YouTube is also looking for feedback and additional resources from teachers to more effectively deliver appropriate content and enhance its offerings.

A distant cousin of YouTube, TeacherTube offers an online community for the sharing of instructional videos. Videos are vetted and so are "safe" for student viewing. It has many teacher- and student-developed videos designed to instruct. What both TeacherTube and YouTube offer are nearly endless viewing opportunities to spur discussions, use as prompts in writing or as debate topic primers, broaden students' knowledge base, expose students to new ideas and perspectives, see what other students think from around the world, and more. These things can all be done while offering the information to students in a medium that they are increasingly reliant on and very familiar with.

Reading to find out more details and to answer questions is particularly well served by technology. Instead of just reading along if you want to know where the location mentioned in a book is, you can use GoogleEarth or MapQuest to find it. Some people have taken this seriously and created links to locations. You can find these at http://googlelittrips.com. For stories in which place or the journey is important, these digital versions can ground the reader in the geography of the place, helping them to feel they are there with the characters.

Viewing for Understanding

The more you use video to prompt class discussion, introduce ideas, present alternative viewpoints, take students to remote locations, learn from other cultures, and make interesting homework assignments, the more you will want good sources of video. Fortunately, there are a variety of different collections that are searchable and usually appropriate for students. From *Movie Archive* (http://archive.org/movies/movies.php) to Apple's Learning Interchange (www.apple.com/education) you can find videos that are focused on content, on how to teach, on how to think about teaching, and much more.

CCSS Connection

- Evaluate the advantages and disadvantages of using different mediums (e.g., print or digital text, video, multimedia) to present a particular topic or idea.

Here is a listing of some of our favorite video sites:

- Media Channel (www.mediachannel.org/): Scroll down to the middle of this page to find an extensive list of links. Many, but not all, link to video clips. Some cannot be downloaded, but the items that are available cover a range of interesting current topics.
- Exploration in Education (www.stsci.edu/exined): This site offers electronic tutorials from a NASA-supported program.
- Apple Learning Interchange (www.apple.com/education/): Videos as well as the ways teachers have incorporated them into the classroom are scattered throughout this site. Lesson plans and study guides can be downloaded as well.
- Perseus Project (www.perseus.tufts.edu/hopper/): This site contains a video about the ancient Olympic games; also take a look at the other collections offered here.
- Edutopia (edutopia.org): This site, produced by the George Lucas Educational Foundation, contains a Video Gallery where leaders in the field of education discuss topics relevant to today's classrooms.
- The Prelinger Archives (https://archive.org/details/prelinger): This site offers over 45,000 advertising, educational, industrial, and amateur films. Since its beginning in 1983, its goal has been to collect, preserve, and facilitate access to films of historic significance that haven't been collected elsewhere. The collection is open to all for free downloading and reuse, but the videos cannot be shown commercially.

Locate, or have students find, written instructions and an informational video on the same topic. They can choose from DIY (do-it-yourself) videos to expert videos on subjects from archery to joinery. Ask them to compare the two ways of communicating how to do something. What are the strengths of each? What are the weaknesses? Which one do they prefer? Why?

Take this idea into film by having students read a book that has been made into a movie. What are the strengths of each version? How does the film deal with the text? Are things left out, added, or portrayed through a different method (showing instead of telling)? What does the visual medium require? What can't be portrayed in a film as well as in a book? Are the differences similar to letter writing versus FaceTime or Skype? How is video fundamentally different? Since we can have video and FaceTime, will they replace text? Middle and high school students enjoy these discussions, and at the same time they deepen their understanding of how the medium conveys its message.

The style of the news media in the United States has varied at different times in our history. At times the news media had a more "objective" style, trying to report the facts to the best of their ability, maintaining a neutral position, and interviewing those on both sides of an issue. At other times, the media have been used to further political agendas, sometimes explicitly, and at other times stating they are reporting the facts while presenting a biased point of view with a lot of attitude or, on news broadcasts, having guest commentators with strong opinions. Have students compare current broadcasts of the same event on at least three different television or radio stations. What do they say? How do they say it? What is the overall message they convey about the topic? Is it a neutral position or a biased one? Students find it interesting when they begin to dissect the content, the tone, and the attitude in a broadcast.

Critical Viewing

As you explore the video collections, consider using them to develop critical viewing skills in students. For each video, explore what is being shown. What is the creator's intent? How are the video and audio used together to accomplish that intent? What camera techniques are used? What is their intent and their actual effect? Ask students to come up with criteria for what makes video effective, entertaining, interesting, thought provoking, or educational and apply them to different videos. Do their analyses agree? If not, in what ways are they different?

To start off, have students analyze video in the same way they would text—ask them to identify the main idea and details. The main idea is often more subtly given in video than in text with more details; some details are stated in the narration, and others are only shown visually. Is there a point of view or perspective? Are there multiple sources of information? What conclusions can be drawn from the piece? Is anything missing? Have students summarize the main idea and details and then post their analyses in a common workspace to compare them.

CCSS Connection

- Analyze the extent to which a filmed or live production of a story or drama stays faithful to or departs from the text or script, evaluating the choices made by the director or actors.

- Integrate and evaluate multiple sources of information presented in different media or formats (e.g., visually, quantitatively) as well as in words in order to address a question or solve a problem.

To study the visual methods in a video, play the same video multiple times, each time having students focus on a different aspect. First, have students close their eyes. What are the qualities of the sound? Is it all the same volume? Is it speech, song, music, or sound effects? What images does the sound evoke? For the next viewing, turn off the sound, and have them focus on the "macro" visuals, such as the background or setting, the movement in the setting, the key characters, and the way they move. What do they see? How would they describe it? What does this layer contribute to the video as a whole? For the third viewing, have students focus on the "micro" images, the small details. Keep the sound off and have them look deeper at the colors of things, the facial expressions, the close-ups. What do they contribute? For the last viewing, let students watch and hear everything. Challenge them to identify yet more elements they did not see or hear before. They may notice the quick cuts, the camera angles, and when close-ups are used versus wide-angle shots and pans. This is both fun and challenging, and students are amazed at what they miss in a single viewing. It makes them more aware of the complexity of video and the role of individual elements in the meaning. This is a good comprehension strategy to use with any video. We find students really like the challenge of looking for new information in each viewing.

Consider having students compare videos based on fact with those based on opinion. You can provide links to the videos to focus their attention on the analysis, rather than on searching for the video. They will need to do fact checks, find several sources that are similar, look at opposing viewpoints, and perhaps make their own video incorporating both facts and a variety of opinions on the topic. This works well with unsolved mysteries in history or with topics in science where facts and opinions collide.

Video can be classified into genres in much the same way as text can. Is the piece a narrative, telling a story? Many video clips online now are informative; others want to persuade the audience of a point of view. Some seem to be informative, but are really persuasive. Documentary-type videos seek to accurately portray a situation. Others are more like historical fiction in being based on something real, but filling in with fictional details. A lot of videos online are entertainment with music that supports the visuals, or are music videos where the video supports the music. Thinking about genre is another way for students to be critical viewers. Have students post a link or show their favorite video and describe it in as many ways as they can from a literary genre standpoint.

What is the effect of video on you? How does it achieve this effect? Start this discussion with students' favorite videos from several genres. Then compare them with the worst videos in the same genres. What makes the first ones effective? Can they affect people differently? These critical viewing discussions lay the groundwork for students' own productions, both in your class and beyond.

E-Readers—AKA E-Books or Electronic Books

Whether or not you own an e-reader like an iPad, Kindle, Nook, Kobo, or Sony Reader, you are likely familiar with them (Figure 7.5). E-readers, or e-books as they are sometimes called, have emerged into the vast market of technology tools available today and seem to be here to stay. They are relatively inexpensive, widely available, easy to use, and lightweight, and they have a long battery life. E-readers are similar to tablet computers without the higher

Figure 7.5 Variety of e-readers

resolution screen that comes with a much higher cost. The lower screen resolution makes them better for reading in all light levels and extends the battery life. Most E-readers have built-in Wifi capability, enabling instant download of new reading material, including books, newspapers, magazines, and more.

The idea of using e-readers in the classroom is not a new one. With the rising cost of text-books and the difficulty of getting timely updates, e-readers and e-books have become a viable option for schools. You may want to invest in an e-reader to learn more about them. You can also encourage your students to use their own personal e-readers if they have one. Schools faced with making a decision about using e-readers in their classrooms must be able to answer three critical questions:

- Which e-reader is the best fit for us?
- How will the e-readers be utilized?
- How will using the e-readers benefit students?

So, let us explore these three questions to help learn more about e-readers. There are a number of factors involved in the decision whether to use them, including cost, use, durability, expandability, and available text. Looking at a e-reader review is a good place to find information on cost, battery life, usability, available titles, and many more interesting comparisons. For 2012, a very good review could be found at http://ebook-reader-review.toptenreviews.com. A Google search with the terms "comparing" and "e-readers" found this site. An update is likely to follow as readers are reviewed and new ones introduced. Most people want something that is durable, nicely priced, and well reviewed and has a built-in web browser.

As you use any technology, you discover new ways to use it. This is true with e-readers. One use is simple: Encourage students to read. Using the new technology can be inspirational for some. Most e-readers have built-in dictionaries that allow the user to place the cursor on a word and the definition appears. This can help with reading comprehension. Textbooks, novels, and short stories are widely available, and some can be downloaded for free from organizations like the CK-12 Foundation and Project Gutenberg (http://instr.iastate.libguides.com/content.php?pid=405430&sid=3321008). Both the Nook from Barnes and Nobel and the Kindle from Amazon offer free electronic content as well.

Expanded vocabulary comes from reading, and anything that encourages students to read is a great addition. The technology may be more engaging for students, and student engagement and learning are closely aligned. Students using e-readers have a great deal of information available to them through the e-reader itself and the connectivity of the device to the Internet. Finding an answer without having to use multiple physical sources can make learning more efficient and students more likely to look up definitions. E-readers also allow students of different abilities to access information and text at their own pace and to find reading materials that are personally interesting. The ability of the e-readers to support an individualized approach makes them a very powerful learning tool. Text size is also adjustable, making them accessible to readers who have difficulty seeing. Many e-readers can also read the text out loud (via a headset), which is helpful for emerging readers to read along with. Having text-to-speech audio functions may also help students with vision problems, language barriers, and a lack of reading fluency.

Summary

To develop students' visual literacy, have them dissect, analyze, and compare video examples. When you give them activities that make their thinking visible, they develop new ways of looking at video, using it, and appreciating it. When they discover the elements of video, they develop new ways of learning from visual material. By comparing good and bad examples, they become more critical consumers and ultimately better producers.

8 Technology Tools for Producing

Producing is the natural continuation of students' mastery of visual imagery. Students who are ready to produce their own viewable content have spent time mastering speaking, listening, and viewing and are now ready to combine these skills into original works. Fortunately, many resources are available that can help students do just this.

In this chapter, we focus on the ways current technology can help students produce original work that supports your classroom goals. We try to separate out activities that focus on producing as the outcome. Students engaged in production as the learning objective are more likely to be highly motivated and involved, task focused, and engaged while, at the same time, developing their research skills, working in teams, deepening their understanding of the content, and thinking carefully about how to communicate with their audiences (Litchfield, Dyson, Wright, Pradhan, & Courtille, 2010). They are often motivated by wanting to produce something, so they are more attentive to instruction on how to communicate effectively.

A paper written by Yochai Benkler (2005) illustrates some of the many possible ways producing content can benefit both students and their audiences. In his paper, Yochai writes about a trip with his kids to South Street Seaport in New York to see a replica of a Viking ship that had sailed to the East Coast from across the Atlantic following the path of Leif Ericson's voyage. The visit inspired his sons to learn more after they got home, and to do so they turned to the Internet. What they found were a wide variety of resources, including what Yochai refers to as "peer-produced" resources. These resources are developed by those actively engaged in learning about a particular topic and are shared as part of being a member of that interested group. When a photographer, motivated solely by his own interest, decides to photograph and record images of Viking ships and then shares them on the Internet, he is participating in a global community comprised of those interested in Viking ships, including Yochai's children, who want to learn more about the Vikings. Finding these peer-produced videos can inspire students to produce their own.

It is fun and exciting for students to share what they know, what they can do, what they are learning, what they care about (or despise), what they are inspired by, or what they are driven to solve. We see this everywhere on the Internet—people expressing ideas, sharing knowledge, and asking questions. Communities of people come together virtually to collaborate, share information and ideas, and talk about things they are struggling to learn or find moving or important. Producing gives students the opportunity to join a community of like-minded people from around the world. Through sharing, they engage in the continuous building of the world's body of knowledge from both experts and amateurs with experience or interest.

In this chapter we look at five strategies for using video technology that are useful for helping students engage in producing their own works:

- Recapping for Understanding
- Creating Video Thank You Notes
- Recording School History
- Bringing Motion and Meaning to Still Images
- Producing Expert Talks

You may want to begin by considering what technologies you have freely available to you. Capturing video can be done with the built-in camera on a computer and most cell phones, and with a video camera if you happen to have access to one. Video cameras come at all different cost levels, and many interesting projects have been done utilizing the $50 flip video cameras that are now widely available. So, while we discuss different ways of producing with video, keep in mind that not all video is shot with a video camera in a traditional sense or edited using sophisticated software.

Recapping for Understanding

Have students create their own 60-second recap of a piece of writing they have read. This website (www.60secondrecap.com) has a library of 60-second recaps of books such as *1984*, *Animal Farm*, *Beowulf*, and *Catcher in the Rye*. If you don't see a title you are looking for, you can request a recap. In "ClubRecap" students can create a login, watch a video with tips and tricks, and review the main ideas behind a recap (themes, motifs, symbols, allegory, metaphors, subtext, and protagonist). That video shares three rules of producing a recap:

- Rule #1: Keep it simple. State the main point up front and explain it.
- Rule #2: Keep it friendly. Talk like you would talk to a friend, and use lots of examples.
- Rule #3: Be yourself. You have a unique perspective to share, so relax and share.

Pass this on to students to get them started:

What can you say in 60 seconds? The Recap website suggests the following steps:

- Read your book. Write out your main idea. Then get picky—pick and choose your best ideas for leading your viewer to that main idea.
- Look for one or two best examples that are easy to understand.
- Start your script. First, recap with the main idea in a way that gets your viewer's attention. How do you want to say it? Be clever or funny to grab the viewer's attention. Think about how a headline gets your attention.

- Consider using props to make your points, be funny, and get the viewer's attention.

- Use graphics to reinforce your point, highlight an important point, surprise your viewer, or keep your viewer interested. Be careful not to let your graphics be distracting, overwhelm your message, or crowd you out.

- Record and upload.

In "RecapResources," students will find a dictionary of terms, how to write a paper, and how to make their own 60-second recap, all in 60-second videos. Students create their own 60-second recaps and add them to their YouTube accounts, filling in the YouTube URL, title, and comment. They choose the topic (cultural context, genre, historical context, major and minor characters, motifs, plot, point of view, setting, symbols, themes, tone) and then type in the name of the book.

CCSS Connection

- Use technology, including the Internet, to produce and publish writing and to interact and collaborate with others.

The 60-second recaps on the website only tackle one topic so students who read the same book might team up to create recaps on different topics and aspects of the book and serve as critical friends for each other. Then their recaps can serve as resources or even sneak previews for other students who have not yet read the book. If you have teams that create recaps of reading assignments, they can compare them and vote their own "best of" the group. Through comparing their recaps they pay closer attention to the key ideas and learn how to recap them accurately.

Creating Video Thank You Notes

Sometimes, students need to send thank you notes to a class visitor or speaker. Other times, they need to send requests. Students can utilize existing technologies to do this in unique and exciting ways. Simply using a camera-enabled computer, students can use YouTube to send video cards, comments, messages, and greetings. Viewers can leave video responses to these messages. It can be challenging for students to speak clearly and articulately. Before recording their message, students will need to script their response, rehearse, get feedback, rewrite, and edit. Video messaging is an activity that relies on a meaningful task so students care about what they are communicating.

Consider having students speak in character from a novel, historical situation, or current event. They could also record a video segment as a commentator on an event, a critic, or observer. You may want to give them a choice of what perspective to take, while stressing that the segment must demonstrate their insight and understanding of the situation.

Using the Technology—YouTube

While we are sure that you have heard of YouTube and likely looked at some piano-playing cat or caught up with your favorite moments from *American Idol*, you may not be familiar with creating videos for YouTube or building your own channel.

Our Student Provocateurs homepage on YouTube is shown in Figure 8.1.

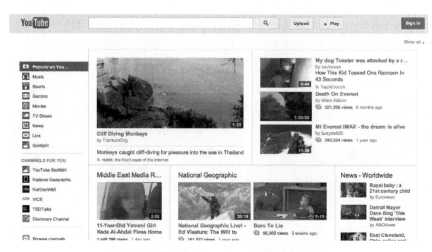

Figure 8.1 Student page on YouTube

Getting started is fairly simple. If you have a Google account already, then you are just about finished—Google, after all, owns YouTube now. If not, don't worry; it is easy to set up a Google account. First, go to YouTube.com and click on the "Create an Account" link near the top and the left. If you have a Google account, it will prompt you to log into your Google account. If not, it will prompt you to create one.

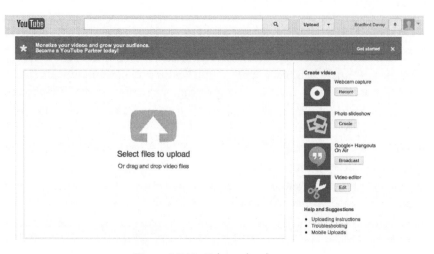

Figure 8.2 YouTube upload page

Once you have created your own channel on YouTube, you can subscribe to other channels that you like, find informative, or feel are just fun. There are a variety of all of these types of channels. Publishing your own work to your YouTube channel is also easy. The hard part is making something worth posting. Once you have something you want to share with the world, open your YouTube account. Click on the "Upload" link at the upper right of the page. This will open an upload window that will instruct you to choose the file you want to upload. A recently added feature allows you to record a video directly from your computer's webcam. A word of caution: There is no editing if you choose to do it this way, so be sure to practice before recording. The upload screen is shown in Figure 8.2.

Recording School History

A favorite day where Brad once taught was the 100th day of school. While these activities relating to the 100th day are mostly for a younger audience, they could be adapted to any age of student. Have students film some of the many 100th day activities, including building a cake out of 100 Munchkins, reading their favorite 100 books, constructing charts and graphs of 100 things, or telling 100 jokes. Whatever you decide to film, first develop a rough schedule so the students will know what is happening that day; then have students write scripts where necessary and, finally, rehearse on days 98 and 99. They can then show their finished products to the rest of the school on day 150 or 200. If the students record the reading of their 100 favorite stories, they might want to offer these videos to the younger grades to view throughout the rest of the year or get them entered into the library as an official resource.

CCSS Connection

- Integrate and evaluate multiple sources of information presented in different media or formats (e.g., visually, quantitatively) as well as in words in order to address a question or solve a problem.

Older students can research important events that happened on each of the 100 days and present them in sound bites (under a minute) on a website to celebrate the day. Roving reporters can report on school events, students' thoughts and comments, and what they learned on each of the 100 days. There can be 100 reporters covering one day each or 30 reporters covering three to four days each, depending on the number of students.

Bringing Motion and Meaning to Still Images

Introduce students to the "Ken Burns effect." Used by documentary maker Ken Burns, it is now a software effect in software programs such as iMovie and Final Cut. It allows students to use still images to tell a story in a more interesting way by panning and zooming around still photos to make certain points and keep the viewers' interest. Challenge students to find five to eight photos to illustrate a point and then add narration accompanied by zooming in and panning around each photo. You can also provide the photos and then have students compare their interpretations, narratives, and choices of focal points to go deeper into the topic. Some tools such as Kizoa (www.kizoa.com) have animation of other kinds and the ability to add special effects.

Producing Expert Talks

Have students prepare a talk about an important idea as if they were presenting it to a large audience, like a TED talk. In preparation, go to www.ted.com/talks to choose a TED talk related to what you are teaching as a model to show the students. You can search for specific words or phrases to help narrow down the selection. The ratings section is also helpful in choosing talks for specific audiences. If nothing seems closely enough related to what you are teaching, make your selection based on what you think will interest your students. Since you will be using the TED talk as a model for how to do this kind of thoughtful, large-group presentation of ideas, the topic of the example you choose is less important than engaging the students. Show it several times—the first time to let them enjoy learning, the second time to take notes on the structure of the talk, and the third time to analyze the presentation. For homework, suggest they find other TED talks to view and dissect in a similar way. Then have them prepare their scripts and videotape the talks, in front of a live audience if possible. Afterward, they can review their own videotape and critique it, as well as view each other's talks. We think Pranav Mistry's "The Thrilling Potential of SixthSense Technology"

(www.ted.com/talks/pranav_mistry_the_thrilling_potential_of_sixthsense_technology.htm) is a good TED talk for middle school and Keith Barry's "Brain Magic" (www.ted.com/talks/keith_barry_does_brain_magic.html) for high school.

Summary

Producing makes students more critical consumers. They also learn more about the topic of their productions because they have to think very carefully about what to include and how to portray it. These "digital natives" are eager to have a voice in the virtual world and need practice in producing more than "one-offs" that they do quickly without editing. While their immersion in digital media means their instincts for what works are pretty good, they can benefit from the discussion and reflection that happen in a classroom setting. Make this kind of work an out-of-school project with frequent touchstones for review and discussion in the classroom. Consider holding screenings, gallery walks, or other showcasing events for student work. Have feedback mechanisms for these events too, such as "best of" for content, technique, engagement, and the like for the audience to vote on.

9 | Using Technology for Viewing and Producing

Addressing the importance of multimodality for life in the 21st century, Kress (2003) observed that digital technologies afford learners more than traditional media and are accelerating and intensifying the move from a single view of literacy to a view based on "multimodal literacy practices." In other words, new media are capable of conveying visual, aural, and kinetic information as well as linguistic meaning. New forms of communication and representation created by these new media enlarge the scope and nature of what it means to be literate.

Literacy for the 21st century goes beyond phonics, phonemics, decoding, encoding, and synthesizing from printed media. Students need to be confident working with digital audio and video. Effectively incorporating technology into classroom literacy activities can significantly enhance attention, motivation, and understanding (Litchfield et al., 2010). When urban high school students were asked to document photographically "what they perceived as the purposes of, impediments to, and supports for their school success" (Zenkov and Harmon, 2009, p. 575), they were highly engaged and motivated, producing highly impactful photographic documentaries.

While the use of technology may be highly motivating to students, it is still necessary to help guide their experience toward educationally relevant outcomes. With multimedia, teachers and students have the opportunity to intentionally recognize communication systems beyond traditional print-based modes. Learners can begin to think about the independent and interrelated ways different design elements can function to communicate a comprehensive message. You can ask questions that help students make intentional use of design elements as they plan, develop, and evaluate their productions using multiple media. The goal of this instruction is threefold: Students will (1) learn the content well enough to communicate it, (2) use media to communicate the content effectively, and (3) to be able to explain how the media choices were made.

In this chapter we combine what we have discussed about viewing with what we have presented about producing to consider what students might accomplish by utilizing these two skills in concert using the following four strategies:

- Answering student questions
- Exploring new ways of doing
- Creating directions and guides
- Developing multimodal presentations

Answering Student Questions

Students are always asking how to do things, from completing homework and reading maps to properly weighing materials for a chemistry experiment. For "how to" learning, have students show their understanding by developing a recorded quick tip guide. There are plenty of models on the Internet from silly to serious; some are wildly creative, and others are extremely effective (students can search for DIY or do-it-yourself, or "how to"). Have student search for how-to videos on topics they know something about, critique them, and, in doing so, develop criteria for what they think makes a good how-to video. This can be done as a class or in small groups, and then compared to create a class version. Then students can themselves create how-to videos to demonstrate comprehension.

A colleague of ours once used this technique to have students make a video production of the classic, "How to Make a Peanut Butter Sandwich." Students came up with some very creative versions of this common task. But don't think this activity is limited to physical tasks. Consider topics such as "how to make a democracy," "how to write a short story," or "how to make a friend."

Students are also always asking what words mean. Wordia (wordia.com) offers definitions of many words with a twist—video definitions by users. Have students identify a word that does not yet have a video definition on Wordia and create one. They can type in the word and if there is no video.

By creating and recording definitions, they are simultaneously developing their vocabulary, communication, and technology skills while contributing to a collection of meaningful products that extends beyond your classroom and school. Consider having students identify what they think are the important words that need to be defined on a topic and then have them create the videos for the words, putting the word in the context of the larger topic and perhaps even referring to other words so viewers can see all the relevant words for that topic or concept.

Exploring New Ways of Doing

Sometimes, finding a new way to do everyday things renews our interest and can lead to additional learning. Have you tried video email? Eyejot (eyejot.com) offers users the ability to send and receive video email using their personal computer and an Internet connection. Eyejot uses its own server so the new video mail does not get loaded down with video spam. While the applications for this technology are not yet fully realized, it does suggest a future in which our students will be able to communicate through speech. Students could effectively learn from sharing messages through video email. Seeing and hearing a fellow student offer information provides a unique set of production and comprehension challenges not associated with the written word.

One of our kids' favorite books when they were very little was *Milo and the Magic Stones*. In this story, Milo, a mouse living on an island with other mice, goes into a dark cave for the winter and discovers magical, glowing stones that provide warmth. Once the other mice see his stone, they all want stones of their own. An elder mouse cautions that they must give something to the island in return for taking a stone for themselves. What the kids enjoyed most was being able to choose the ending of the story: either happy or sad. Taking this even further, your students could choose their own ending for something you are reading. By producing their own ending, they are able to add their own ideas; then they can share what they have produced in a video email to you, which you can then share with the class or post on a private class workspace.

Creating Directions and Guides

Often, to answer the questions students ask repeatedly, teachers will develop directions, help sheets, or notes that attempt to guide students. Screencast-O-Matic (screencast-o-matic.com) is an online screen/browser recorder for recording anything that is on your computer's screen. The free version gives you up to 15 minutes of recording time. This tool can be used to record web-page navigation directions or other web-specific instructions for students to follow. Either use it yourself to develop lessons for students and guide their learning, or have students develop their own directions to help other students navigate a website, research a topic, play an online game, enter information into a form, post a blog comment, or show their thinking while researching using the Internet. Teachers like to use this website to record mini-lectures as they advance through a slide show or browse useful websites.

Using the Technology—Screencast-O-Matic

Screencast-O-Matic has made getting started using its free online software about as easy as it gets. Going to the homepage, you will see something like Figure 9.1.

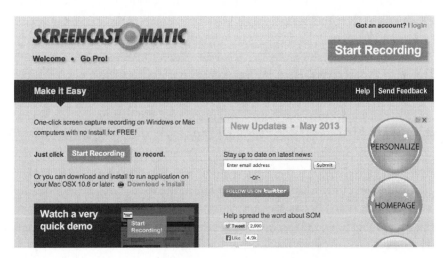

Figure 9.1 Screencast-O-Matic homepage

What you need to do now is just click the "Start Recording" button and you are off and running. Clicking this button will launch the S-O-M capture frame that allows you to align what is to be captured on your screen. Once you get this set just the way you want it, you can start recording by clicking the red record button at the far left of the control bar that appears with the capture frame. You can pause the recording as necessary if you are launching a new page to record, opening a different document, or rearranging things on your screen. You can also record your voice while showing things on the screen. This works best with a micro-phone or a headset with a built-in microphone. Be sure to check your volume level before you start. Once you are finished recording, click "Done." Clicking "Done" opens the video you just recorded into a preview window.

The preview page lets you view the video you captured and hear the audio you recorded. If you are happy with what you have, you have three choices: (1) publish to the S-O-M website, (2) publish directly to YouTube, or (3) publish as a video file that gets downloaded to your desktop. Choosing "Done with this Recording" deletes the video and takes you back to the homepage.

Students also enjoy making "how to" videos that show them taking the viewer through their favorite video game or online site. In the beginning it may be necessary that they start on a high-interest topic to get them hooked on the tool. Then may choose to use it for school projects in other classes. Making a video gives them a chance to work on honing their presentation skills. They may also want to develop an accompanying written description. The advantage of the writ-ten piece is that the user can review the entire piece or portions of it at his or her own pace.

Have students create study guides for required reading using Screencast-O-Matic. This is also a good tool to show how they solved problems from start to finish because it can include audio and text. Additional ideas for using Screencast-O-Matic include presenting online lessons for the class and developing them for diverse users, giving homework assignments, having students use it to demonstrate their learning and capturing it for assessment, demonstrating research methods as you search the web for information, or sending a link to parents so that they can see what the class is doing and learn how to involve themselves.

Developing Multimodal Presentations

While still in its early stages, research has begun to show significant increases in student learn-ing when visual and verbal multimodal learning is occurring (Cisco, 2008). Multimodal often describes the interplay of multiple forms of learning combined to enhance the experience for the learner. In order to deeply understand a topic, learners not only need to know relevant facts, theo-ries, and applications, but they must also make sense of the topic through organization of those ideas into a framework (schema) of understanding. Students develop schema most effectively when what they are trying to learn is something meaningful to them and combines more than one form of information—auditory, visual, movement.

CCSS Connection

- Use technology, including the Internet, to produce and publish writing and to interact and collaborate with others.
- Produce clear and coherent writing in which the development, organization, and style are appropriate to task, purpose, and audience.

Watching our students, we recognize that they combine and move fluidly between multi-modal forms of learning. Looking for ways to help students incorporate different technologies in their products is one way of helping them learn. VoiceThread allows group conversations to be collected in one place and shared from anywhere. VoiceThreads are multimedia slide shows that contain images, documents, and videos and allow people to navigate slides and leave comments using voice, text, audio files, or video. Building a VoiceThread is easy and fairly intuitive. As with most technologies, your students will get it right away. An additional feature is that the thread can be moderated for materials and comments by the teacher and other students, giving students the opportunity to learn collaboratively by moderating their own discussions.

The VoiceThread site has many examples of how teachers are using it, including one in which viewers can respond to photographs of Chernobyl and the stories of the contamination and the people who lived there. Another thread has simple math problems such as "38 + 61." Students respond with their solutions. All the solutions are available as thumbnails for clicking so students can see and hear everyone else's solutions. Another thread is a book review, in which the slides are pictures from the book. The creator of the VoiceThread summarizes the action associated with each illustration and adds a personal reflection. Others can add comments to each slide.

Key ideas

- Today's learners are immersed in a very visually stimulating media world.
- Images are highly engaging and convey large amounts of information, perhaps providing the experience closest to daily life.
- Children between the ages of 8 and 18 are exposed to an average of 10 hours of media daily (TV, music, computers, and video games); it is estimated that nearly 60% have a TV in their bedroom.
- Visual literacy standards have evolved to help teachers direct student learning and have been adopted by 49 states.
- Proficiency in 21st-century visual literacy includes developing skills with the tools of technology, designing and sharing information, managing, analyzing, and synthesizing multiple streams of simultaneous information and creating, critiquing, analyzing, and evaluating multimedia tasks.
- Proficiency in visual literacy also includes understanding how and why media messages are constructed, examining how individuals interpret messages differently, and understanding how media can influence beliefs and behaviors.
- Producing visual material is a natural continuation of mastering understanding of visual imagery.

Summary

When thinking about projects that involve viewing and producing, have students collaborate to review and critique examples so they can come up with criteria for their own productions. Then as they share their productions, encourage them to be critical friends to each other. When all their works are visible to each other, they learn through each other's perspectives, making the conversation richer and deeper than individual students responding privately. When they come together they have the benefit of having seen everyone's work so their understanding and discussion expand beyond their individual perspectives.

References for Section III

Aristotle. (1941). On memory and reminiscence. In *The basic works of Aristotle* (W. Rhys. McKeon, Trans.). New York: Random House.

Baker, F. (2012). *Communication: Viewing*. Retrieved January 2012 from www.frankwbaker.com/ ela_elaboration.htm.

Beilke, J., & Stuve, M. (2004). A teacher's use of digital video with urban middle school students: Expanding definitions of representational literacy. *Teacher Educator, 39*(3), 157–169.

Benkler, Y. (2005). *Common wisdom: Peer production of educational materials*. Center for Open and Sustainable Learning at Utah State University. Retrieved January 2012 from www.benkler. org/Common_Wisdom.pdf.

Benson, P. (1997). Problems in picturing text: A study of visual/verbal problem solving. *Technical Communication Quarterly, 6*(2), 141–160.

Buckingham, D., & Harvey, I. (2001). Imagining the audience: Language, creativity and communication in youth media production. *Journal of Educational Media, 26*(3), 173–184.

Cisco. (2008). *Multimodal learning through media: What the research says*. Retrieved January 2012 from www.cisco.com/web/strategy/docs/education/Multimodal-Learning-Through-Media.pdf.

de Block, L., & Rydin, I. (2006). Digital rapping in media productions: Intercultural communication through youth culture. In D. Buckingham & R. Willett (Eds.), *Digital generations: Children, young people, and new media* (pp. 295–312). Mahwah, NJ: Lawrence Erlbaum.

Dondis, D. (1973). *A primer of visual literacy*. Cambridge, MA: MIT Press.

Frey, N., & Fisher, D. (2008). *Teaching visual literacy: Using comic books, graphic novels, anime, cartoons, and more to develop comprehension and thinking skills*. New York: Corwin Press.

Georgia Department of Education (2013). *English Language Arts 6–8*. Retried from www. georgiastandards.org/Common-Core/Pages/ELA-6-8.aspx

Grace, D., & Tobin, J. (2002). Butt jokes and mean-teacher parodies: Video production in the elementary classroom. In David Buckingham (Ed.), *Teaching popular culture media, education, and culture* (7–18). Bristol, PA: Taylor & Francis.

Hull, G., & Nelson, M. (2005). Locating the semiotic power of multimodality. *Written Communication, 22*(2), 224–261.

Jones-Kavaller, B., & Flannigan, S. (2006). Connecting the digital dots: Literacy of the 21st century. *Educause Quarterly, 2*, 7–9.

Kress, G. (2003). *Literacy in the new media age*. New York: Routledge.

Litchfield, A., Dyson, L., Wright, M., Pradhan, S., & Courtille, B. (2010, July). *Student-produced vodcasts as active metacognitive learning.* Paper presented at the Advanced Learning Technologies (ICALT), 2010 IEEE 10th International Conference. Retrieved January 2012 from http://ieeexplore.ieee.org/xpl/freeabs_all.jsp?arnumber=5572517.

Metros, S., & Woolsey, K. (2006). Visual literacy: An institutional imperative. *Educause Review, 41*(3), 80–81.

Nielsen. (2009). *How teens use media.* Retrieved January 3, 2012, from http://blog.nielsen.com/nielsenwire/reports/nielsen_howteensusemedia_june09.pdf.

Niesyto, H., Buckingham, D., & Fisherkeller, J. (2003). Video culture: Crossing borders with young people's video productions. *Television & New Media, 4*(4), 461–482.

Stokes, S. (2001). Visual literacy in teaching and learning: A literature perspective. *Electronic Journal for the Integration of Technology in Education, 1*(1). Retrieved April 20, 2009, from http://ejite.isu.edu/Volume1No1/Stokes.html.

Tapscott, D. (1997). *Growing up digital: The rise of the net generation.* New York: McGraw-Hill.

Wang, C.C. (2001). Photovoice ethics: Perspectives from Flint Photovoice. *Health Education & Behavior, 28*(5), 560–572.

Zenkov, K., & Harmon, J. (2009, April). Picturing a writing process: Photovoice and teaching writing to urban youth. *Journal of Adolescent & Adult Literacy, 52*(7), 575–584.

Multi-Literacies (multimodal)

A computer does not substitute for judgment any more than a pencil substitutes for literacy.
—Robert McNamara

In this section we discuss how reading, writing, speaking, listening, viewing, and producing images come together in a multi-literacy environment. After an introduction to multi-literacies, Chapter 10 examines projects and how emerging educational technologies have developed opportunities to reach every student in a unique way. Chapter 11 looks at how the social nature of learning has grown considerably with the introduction of 21st-century technologies into the classroom. Chapter 12 is designed to help you, the classroom teacher, to develop your own personal learning network for using technology resources, and it provides suggestions for how that network can help you learn and grow along with your students.

Key ideas

- Project-based learning can be used as a powerful learning tool in conjunction with 21st-century technologies.

- Students learn by researching, collecting data, collaborating with their peers, being mentored, and exploring.

- There are many online project sites that can help facilitate project-based learning in the classroom.

- Having work reviewed by peers, stakeholders, and other audiences is a powerful learning tool and intensifies learning.

- Students can publish their ideas for their peers through blogging, document sharing, slide shows, video, writing articles, and local media.

- Group projects work well because students learn from other students when they are in close proximity and have shared goals. Incidental learning goes up because they are paying attention to what is said, retaining what they see and hear to use in the project, copying each other's successful behaviors, and feeling motivated to succeed in front of their peers.

- Keeping up with technology can be a big challenge for any educator—building a personal learning network will help.

Introduction

There are some numbers floating around out there that perhaps you have seen. They suggest that *we remember . . .*

10% *of what we read*
20% *of what we hear*
30% *of what we see*
50% *of what we see and hear*
70% *of what we say . . .*
and **90**% *of what we say and do!*

Unfortunately, these often-quoted learning statistics are, for the most part, unsubstantiated (Cisco Systems, 2008). These numbers have been used in numerous reports and publications beginning with Edgar Dale's (1954) *Audio-Visual Methods in Technology* (see Figure 10.1).

It is interesting to note that in Dale's original diagram, there were no percentages given. Where they came from is anyone's guess. Perhaps they are an elaboration on what Confucius said over 2,000 years ago: "I hear and I forget, I see and I remember, I do and I understand." The diagram and the accompanying percentages continue to be used in current literature, webspaces, and professional materials to encourage higher involvement by students in their own learning. What we can discern and have come to know through careful observation and research is that the greater the abstraction, the less impact on learning. There is an important lesson in this for us all: We must take a more purposeful and academic approach to determining the best ways to help our students learn. What the research has shown is that learning happens over time through

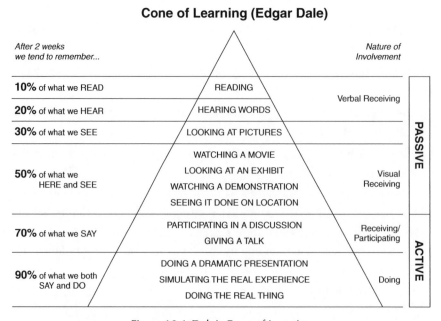

Figure 10.1 Dale's Cone of Learning

complex physiological and cognitive processes (Mayer, 2003), that it happens differently for different learners (Bransford, Brown, & Cocking, 2000), and it is critical to have students think about their ways of thinking.

Bransford and colleagues (2000) outline three important principles critical in the redesign of learning:

1. Student preconceptions of curriculum must be engaged in the learning process.
2. Expertise is developed through deep understanding.
3. Learning is optimized when students use metacognitive strategies.

For the classroom activities, this means the following:

1. Student learning is greatly enhanced when the curriculum (1) requires each student's prior knowledge to be made visible, allowing them to see what they think they already know; (2) gets their prior knowledge out in the open so they can build on it or evolve it; and (3) has activities that challenge old conceptions and create new ways of understanding.
2. Students learn more when the concepts are personally meaningful to them, when they keep pushing to make sense of ideas in the context of their lives and immediate experience, or through immersion in another rich context.
3. Students who are actively thinking about their learning optimize that learning. Ways to think about their learning include trying to predict outcomes, explaining ideas to themselves, making a note of failures and learning from them, and activating their prior knowledge intentionally to optimize their learning.

It is also important to note that recent research on multimedia and modality effects on student learning has supported Dale's Cone of Learning. Findings from these studies suggest that retention is improved when words are accompanied in close proximity by pictures, and that extraneous words, pictures, and sounds distract from learning. Students learn better from narrated media than from read-alongs, and individual learners are affected by the design of the delivery, particularly if they have less prior knowledge and difficulty with spatiality, and if the material is highly complex (Mayer, 2003; McKay, 1999; Moreno & Valdez, 2005). Since the blending of images, words, and sounds is inherent in emerging educational technologies, a careful progression of incorporation and utilization of images, audio, and text is warranted to enhance learning.

This is a tremendous time to be involved in education. This generation of learners not only has an understanding of but also a yearning for learning environments rich with technologies that enhance communication, collaboration, interaction, and engagement. Today's teachers have greater opportunities than ever before for reaching every learner in the classroom in a literacy-rich environment. Addressing multi-literacies, or referring to students directly as multimodal learners (Weir, 2008), has become increasingly necessary and, with the utilization of widely available technologies, increasingly possible.

What have been traditionally described as multiple intelligences (visual, tactile/kinesthetic, and auditory; Gardner, 1993) are still present in the classroom of today in the same numbers. What makes today different is that educators have new tools available to them to meet the needs of this diverse audience. Material that was once limited to what could be "run off" on a ditto is now viewable as an interactive document on a computer (hypertext). What would have taken reams of paper can now be given to each learner electronically (email, List-servs, webpages). What was once read by students is now available as an immersive 3D interactive world experience (River City, Whyville, Quest Atlantis, and Math Blaster—to name a few). Where learners once read about an artist to get to know them, they can now visit that artist at their home and talk with them about their work, and paint side by side with them virtually (Second Life™, 2013—Secondlife.com).

Today's learners have grown up with unprecedented access to information and ideas and have experience with its many forms and functions. They are functionally multi-literate. You can help them become consciously multi-literate by reflecting on the tools, how to use them, and their effects. This section looks at how educators can help their students become metacognitive (to think about multimedia, not just use it) by capitalizing on emerging educational technology and discussing its features, uses, and effects. Going beyond recognizing students as having varied learning styles, multimedia tools can be used in conjunction with sound pedagogy to *empower* learners with different learning styles to find their individual strengths and capitalize on them. Today's learners are tomorrow's leaders, and they will be leading in unique and interesting ways, with technology as a key component of their leadership. What they learn and the exposure they are given while in school will prepare them for success. Today's educators must be able to offer unique and diverse exposure to educational technology tools designed to enhance the learning experience for all learners.

Common Core State Standards for Multi-Literacies

This section identifies the Common Core State Standards for multi-literacies for middle and high school grade bands. The focus is on the integration of ideas. The CCSS have been identified throughout this section.

Integration of Knowledge and Ideas

Grades 6–8

- Integrate quantitative or technical information expressed in words in a text with a version of that information expressed visually (e.g., in a flowchart, diagram, model, graph, or table).

- Distinguish among facts, reasoned judgment based on research findings, and speculation in a text.

- Compare and contrast the information gained from experiments, simulations, video, or multimedia sources with that gained from reading a text on the same topic.

- Write informative/explanatory texts, including the narration of historical events, scientific procedures/ experiments, or technical processes.
  - Introduce a topic clearly, previewing what is to follow; organize ideas, concepts, and information into broader categories as appropriate to achieving purpose; include formatting (e.g., headings), graphics (e.g., charts, tables), and multimedia when useful to aiding comprehension.

○ Use technology, including the Internet, to produce and publish writing and present the relationships between information and ideas clearly and efficiently.

Grades 9–10

● Translate quantitative or technical information expressed in words in a text into visual form (e.g., a table or chart) and translate information expressed visually or mathematically (e.g., in an equation) into words.

● Compare and contrast findings presented in a text to those from other sources (including their own experiments), noting when the findings support or contradict previous explanations or accounts.

● Write informative/explanatory texts, including the narration of historical events, scientific procedures/experiments, or technical processes.

○ Introduce a topic and organize ideas, concepts, and information to make important connections and distinctions; include formatting (e.g., headings), graphics (e.g., figures, tables), and multimedia when useful to aiding comprehension.

○ Use technology, including the Internet, to produce, publish, and update individual or shared writing products, taking advantage of technology's capacity to link to other information and to display information flexibly and dynamically.

Grades 11–12

● Integrate and evaluate multiple sources of information presented in diverse formats and media (e.g., quantitative data, video, multimedia) in order to address a question or solve a problem.

● Synthesize information from a range of sources (e.g., texts, experiments, simulations) into a coherent understanding of a process, phenomenon, or concept, resolving conflicting information when possible.

● Write informative/explanatory texts, including the narration of historical events, scientific procedures/experiments, or technical processes.

○ Introduce a topic and organize complex ideas, concepts, and information so that each new element builds on that which precedes it to create a unified whole; include formatting (e.g., headings), graphics (e.g., figures, tables), and multimedia when useful to aiding comprehension.

○ Use technology, including the Internet, to produce, publish, and update individual or shared writing products in response to ongoing feedback, including new arguments or information.

For updated standards and more information, visit the Common Core State Standards Initiative (www.corestandards.org).

10 | Projects

Just as we have understood for years that different learners learn differently in different situations (Moreno & Mayer, 2007), so, too, do we need to recognize that different technologies address different learners' needs. The diversity of available learning technologies suggests that there are many different ways to approach learning. This diversity allows educators to envision how to best meet the needs of individual learners utilizing these technologies as tools for learning and to give students experiences with different technologies to see what is most supportive of their learning.

One way in which technology can be leveraged to help facilitate student learning is through projects. Project learning, often called project-based learning (PBL), has been around for years (Hmelo-Silver, 2004), and it is likely that you have used it in your classroom already. Project learning is an approach to teaching in which students generate questions concerning real-world problems or challenges. Students usually work in small teams to develop a greater understanding through their research and collaboration, often involving the real-world use of technology. Learning is collaborative, student directed, multidisciplinary, relatively long term, and outcomes based, with student creating products as artifacts of their learning (Barron, 1998).

Project learning in the 21st-century classroom goes beyond basic Internet research projects and so-called Web Quests. Successful projects are designed to encourage student interaction with technology in which students find themselves engaged in a meaningful experience (Boss & Krauss, 2007). An example of a very successful learning project is Generation Yes (GenYES; genyes. org). In GenYES, students are tasked with integrating learning technology into their schools by taking an active role. GenYES describes itself as "the only student-centered research-based solution for school-side technology integration." Working with their teachers, GenYES students design technology-infused lessons and work as classroom-based technology support. Through these efforts, students gain technology and leadership experience while their technology integration efforts benefit the entire school. The projects that students involve themselves in are obtainable, real world, and important to the school, and they give genuine responsibility and importance to the students.

The GenYES project has met with great success and represents a good example of what can be done to involve students with technology in your school and develop their understanding of multi-literacy skills for learning and communicating. This chapter looks at three major areas where projects may have an impact on the literacy of students through the utilization of technology. The first section, *Research, Data Collection, Collaboration, Mentoring, Expeditions, Events,* looks at how different types of projects can be used within the classroom to enhance the ties between school and the broader world of the students. The second section, *Using Online Project Sites*, provides a close look at a few online sites that offer excellent projects for students that utilize technology as a tool for learning. The third section, *An Audience for Learning*, demonstrates the educational importance of having an audience for student work.

Research, Data Collection, Collaboration, Mentoring, Expeditions, Events, Assessment

No one project meets all of the needs of both teachers and students in improving literacy. Often, different projects are undertaken at different times of the year corresponding with how well they enhance the curriculum and align with class work. This section presents seven project types. This list is not designed to be comprehensive. Rather, it is designed to illustrate the variety of project ideas available and encourage you to look further into the topic to find something that works for you, your students, and your curriculum.

Research

While it has been common for students to do Internet searches as part of the class work, these searches often leave students disconnected from the content after the search is over since they have not developed any personal meaning during their research. The International Reading Association has an excellent web resource called "Read Write Think" (readwritethink.org) that offers ways to engage students in online literacy learning. It provides tools that are designed to help students organize their research and write about what they are learning. Taking the time and effort to write creates that deep understanding that Bransford et al. (2000) described. Having tools that allow for a better organization of research, that encourage inquiry and analysis, and that support learning through writing can make a big difference in student understanding.

CCSS Connection

- Distinguish among facts, reasoned judgment based on research findings, and speculation in a text.

One lesson that we have found to be particularly interesting to students and very impactful is called "Audience, Purpose, and Language Use in Electronic Messages." In this lesson, students explore the language of electronic messaging and how it affects other writing, while exploring the creativity of using Internet abbreviations in specific situations and more formal writing in others. To do the activity, have your students give you some of the abbreviations that they use and write them along with their meaning on an overhead or the board. Students may need to look some additional ones up if they are stuck on "LOL" and "FYI." The website Internet

Slang (www.internetslang.com) also offers a pdf that can be used as part of the activity. Give students a sample email to decode by writing out all of the abbreviations (again, there is one to download from the site). Engage students in a discussion of how they might use different language when writing to different audiences. Some scenarios to consider are emailing a college or university as part of an application, emailing a fellow student about something you missed during class, emailing with a friend to catch up, or emailing a thank you letter to a grandparent.

Data Collection

Collecting data is a regular component of much course work and part of an engaging classroom. There are multiple online tools that allow students to organize their collected data in meaningful ways. However, the collection of data goes beyond gathering information; it is a means of thinking through ideas. Collecting data helps students generate ideas, consider different sources in their work, and better organize their thoughts. Data collection is often thought of as a science endeavor. It is easy to picture students standing around a lab bench looking closely at a thermometer and recording their data in a notebook. It is, however, just as likely for members of an English classroom to collect data about a book they are reading or for Spanish students studying the historical context of a regional dialect to collect very informative data over time and across locations. Databases, spreadsheets, and even GIS maps help students collect, organize, and analyze these data.

CCSS Connection

- Integrate quantitative or technical information expressed in words in a text with a version of that information expressed visually (e.g., in a flowchart, diagram, model, graph, or table).

To get started using online data sources, you might find this activity on sea level rise from Data in the Classroom (dataintheclassroom.org) very useful. We particularly like this activity because it offers five levels of increasing complexity when used in a diverse classroom: Entry, Adoption, Adaptation, Interactivity, and Invention. Simply go to Dataintheclassroom.org and follow the link to "Satellite Data." There, they offer a complete teacher's guide, complete lesson plan, links to standards and additional information and resources, tools, and even assessment activities. It is very interesting information and very informative at the same time.

Collaboration

Working in groups is enhanced when students collaborate to solve meaningful problems and learn the importance of working with their peers to accomplish more than they might on their own. There are numerous ways your students can collaborate as part of their class work, and we have discussed a number of those tools in previous sections of the book. To summarize, utilizing a shared workspace such as a Google Group or a wiki can facilitate student collaborations. Collaboration can be encouraged by offering assignments that focus on different student strengths. It is also enhanced by increasing the complexity of the assignments so students need to work together to be successful. With complex assignments, interdependence is necessary and provides a real benefit. There are also collaborative social networks developed through websites like Ning (the online social network space) that are designed just for students of different age groups. They have examples of the types of projects that students are doing around the world and are a great source of ideas and inspiration. Students have also collaborated to raise money to help support others around the world through the micro-loans given out by Kiva (Kiva.org). While not traditionally what comes to mind with the typical classroom collaboration, these kinds of projects offer students the opportunity to help bring about meaningful change in the world with others interested in the same goal.

Mentoring

Mentors continue to have an important role to play in any educational setting. Since the time of Socrates, students have benefited from working closely with a more experienced person. Sometimes, mentors are fellow students, other times they are their teachers, and at still other times they are individuals from the community. The available community has grown much larger as the Internet has come into schools around the world. Now, mentors are available from as close as the student at the next desk to as far as someone on the other side of the world.

Internet mentoring relationships are a cost-effective and convenient way to help students develop relationships with caring adults. One example, out of the University of Arizona, called WISE (Women in Science and Engineering) recruits mentors from the university and surrounding area to work with high school girls interested in careers in science, technology, engineering, or mathematics (STEM) to help promote STEM fields and the girls' interest in related careers as well as support them in their studies. Students and mentors utilize available electronic technologies to connect and share as well as help build their relationship. Science Buddies (www.sciencebuddies.org) is another example of the utilization of technology to help bring together students and working professionals interested in mentoring. Working through Science Buddies, students can get the opportunity to work on current science projects and explore areas of interest.

Expeditions

Expeditions, activities, and learning adventures—whatever you call them—have a role in getting students excited about what they are learning. Exploring a topic gives students the opportunity to find their own meaning, importance, and relevance in what they are learning about. Technology can make the exploration of ideas much more rapid and in depth. Exploring in the research sense takes considerable skill and practice to successfully complete. This is a critical task for 21st-century students to master and one they may not be comfortable or proficient in.

In order to offer effective expeditions/adventures it is important that there be little in the way of negative consequences for "wrong" expeditions. What is meant by "wrong" here is important. Right and wrong play only a small role in developing better understandings and do little to promote an atmosphere of exploration. Encouraging students to explore without negative consequences encourages the growth of a learning environment where students can take risks and not be afraid of being wrong. Remember, the only bad question is the one not asked. Classroom explorations encourage students to seek answers to their questions and reveal their own misconceptions. Consider taking expeditions around your school, out into the schoolyard, or by way of the Internet to anywhere your students may want to go. Encourage them to shape their own experience and find ways to share it with others.

Try this as a first round with classroom explorations—Exploring Your Town. In this activity, students are tasked with finding out about their own town using the Internet as a start. Extensions to this activity include visiting town sites, meeting with town leaders, having town leaders visit your classroom, mapping, exploring historical changes, and more. To start, assign students in pairs to learn about different aspects of their town including its history, leadership, geography, and demographics. Students who live in the same town should be paired together. Students living outside of a town should choose one closest to their home. Once students have gathered all of their information, they should take turns reporting to the rest of the class about what they found out. A master listing of information should be developed from their findings. Once the list is complete, have students talk about what else they might want to know about their town and how they might find that information. Once they have uncovered all of the information about their town, they can make a brochure or website that is designed to promote tourism. Encourage them to add colorful images, interesting information, town personalities, sights, and more.

Events

Tying events happening in your classroom, school, community, or in the world with what your students are doing and learning is a valuable teaching tool. Events can be as global as Earth Day or as local as a talent show. Students will often engage more with a project if it is tied to an event. This typically lends more importance to it and allows the students to make additional connections to things that are important to them. These connections enhance their learning through focusing their attention and getting them interested enough to ask questions and pursue answers. Such motivation will lead them to pursue interesting, complex questions in more depth.

There are some really great topic-specific event webspaces available. A few of the most appealing are NASA's Kids Club, the National Literacy Coalition, and perhaps your local school's website. NASA's Kids Club (www.nasa.gov/audience/forkids/kidsclub/flash/index.html#. UowO8WQkEYh) and the National Literacy Coalition (nationalliteracycoalition.org) offer lists of topic-specific events and ideas about how to incorporate them into your curriculum. Your local town and school websites may offer ideas for projects. By combining a current event with classroom learning, you are making connections to the larger world in which the students already live, enhancing the meaning of what is what they are learning, and often coming up with a built-in audience of stakeholders to use their work. We recently worked with a teachers whose students mapped a greenway with distances, plants, rocks, and questions about sustainability. The information was available on the school website and could be printed with QR codes to obtain more information.

Assessment

There are a wide variety of assessment tools that can make use of technology. Some technology tools for assessment are well tested and in easy and manageable formats. These include rubrics; student portfolio tools; online quizzes, tests, and puzzles; authentic assessment; and online report cards. We discuss rubrics, online quizzes and tests, and electronic portfolios in this subsection—keeping in mind that there are many to consider.

Rubrics

A rubric is a way for the instructor to communicate expectations of quality for a particular task or project. The rubric is made public for all students and can, therefore, be used as a form of ongoing assessment, offering students the opportunity to compare their efforts to the expectations and make improvements as appropriate before resubmitting their work. When developing a rubric, it is important to consider the stages by which students develop an accurate understanding. Each level should describe something positive, an evolving understanding of the criterion. If you have taught something, you generally know what students have difficulty with and what they get first, then what they get next, and so on. These become the levels of the rubric.

In the first rubric (Table 10.1), the levels are written in the first person so students can use it for reflection. Notice how each level is positive. This lets each student see what he or she is doing well and what the next level of proficiency is. In the rubric in Table 10.2, the axes are reversed, with the criteria in the first column and the levels building from left to right.

Steps for Creating a Developmental Rubric

There are many resources available online for rubric development. With a little searching, you may even be able to find a rubric that has been developed for the topic or project you are conducting. If you choose to create your own, here are some steps we have used to create rubrics. Creating a rubric does not have to be difficult if you know the content and use this process:

1. If you can, get together with someone else who also has taught the skill or concept. You may be surprised how similar your experiences will be with naïve conceptions and the stages students go through to develop an accurate understanding of the concept.
2. Make a list of the things you teach about the concept. This list will change, so just get it down in the order you generally teach it. There is no need to wordsmith or try to refine it at this point. This list is the beginning of the criteria list.

Table 10.1 Writing rubric

	Focus	Content	Organization	Style	Conventions
	What is the point of the story?	*What does the reader know from reading what I wrote?*	*How did I tell the story? How did I organize it?*	*What pictures did my writing paint in the reader's mind?*	*What do I need to proof-read for?*
4	The reader knows what my point is about the topic and why I think that.	I choose the most interesting and important ideas to tell the reader in an interesting, fun way to make my point.	I chose to organize it the way I did to be interesting and easy to read.	People can tell that a piece of writing is mine by how I write.	Anyone can read and understand my writing because I use correct spelling, punctuation, and grammar.
3	I make one big point about the topic or idea in the prompt. There are a lot of smaller ideas to support the big idea.	I know what I am talking about and the reader does too after they read what I wrote. It makes my point.	I tell what I know like a story with a beginning, middle, and end connected with transition words.	My readers feel like I am talking to them and they are part of what is happening. I use lots of interesting words and phrases.	When I reread what I wrote, I corrected the spelling, punctuation, and grammar.
2	I chose ideas that go together and tell why I think they go together.	I collected a lot of ideas and used the best ones to make my point.	I thought about how to tell the story so it would make sense to the reader.	I write like I talk. I want readers to understand what I write.	I asked a classmate to read my writing and ask me questions about what wasn't clear to her.
1	I write some ideas about the topic that come into my mind as I write.	I write about some things I have heard about the topic.	I write down what I think in the order I think of it.	I tell what happened in just a few sentences.	I write a bunch of ideas instead of complete sentences. I spell words like I hear them.

Non-scorable: blank, illegible, incoherent, insufficient | Off-prompt: readable but does not respond to prompt

Table 10.2 Rubric in a different format

	1	2	3	4
Focus	*Several ideas in no particular order*	Similar ideas are together	One big idea with some support	Main idea with supporting details
Content	Some things about the topic	Related ideas	Ideas presented to make a point	*Important and interesting ideas add up to make a point*
Organization	Ideas appear as the writer thought of them	Ideas build on each other	Beginning, middle, and end	*Interesting and easy to read with transitions and organizing ideas*
Style	Simple description of topic or events	Written as if the author were speaking	Lots of interesting words and phrases that paint a picture	*Individual style and voice*
Conventions	No use of punctuation	Little attention to conventions	Errors do not distract from the meaning	*Correct spelling, punctuation, and grammar*

3. List each key idea in a column, preferably in a spreadsheet you can project, but using a board or chart paper will do. The students and teacher both need to be able to see the development as it progresses so he or she can contribute.

4. For each criterion, describe the top level, usually a "4." What does good work look like? What does it include?

5. Now, starting with a "1" discuss what learners think they know or can do for each criterion. Think about where these ideas come from and how you generally challenge them. This leads to level "2."

6. Level 2 is what students begin to understand first—the easiest ideas to develop. What is this initial understanding?

7. Level 3 is similar to level 2 in that it captures that next level of understanding. What can you get students to understand next about each key idea? If you're having trouble identifying this level, think about the activities you generally do with students to evolve their understanding.

8. Keep each level description *positive*. Describe what learners *do* understand, not what they don't understand. This helps you to support students in developing the next level of understanding and lets students see what that next level looks like in the rubric.

Online Rubric Tools

iRubric (rcampus.com) is a free comprehensive rubric development, assessment, and sharing tool. Teach-Nology (teach-nology.com) offers a very comprehensive list of rubric maker tools available online as well as a host of pre-made rubrics by subject and project focus.

Online Quizzes and Tests

While quizzes and tests are not our favorite form of assessment, they offer a quick assessment of factual knowledge. Technology tools can make the process of creating, administering, and grading tests easier. There are a number of online quiz and test development and delivery tools. If your school has a digital grade book system, you may even have a quiz and test tool associated with it. Using these tools lets you focus on the content of the questions, capturing those plausible but naïve understandings students have in the multiple choices or in the wording of the open-ended questions.

Most online tools for developing and administering quizzes and tests allow you to create classes, quizzes, and/or tests, administer them, and view the results. You are likely to use a variety of question types, including multiple choice, open response, and essay. These tools all allow you to create these different types of questions and will suggest others as well. You will also be able to attach multimedia files to questions, offer the quiz in multiple languages (great for bilingual classrooms and language classes), access your account from any Internet-connected computer, and allow your students to review the quiz before submitting. You can also make copies and change the question order if you are going to give the same quiz to multiple class sections. The downside is that many of these services cost money—not a huge sum considering the time they can save, but money that most teachers just don't have. So, get your school to pay the $2 to $20/month fee for you! OK, so they are not likely to do that. But consider paying $19.95/year and skipping four lattes and you are even. You can check on your students' evolving understanding and help them become more literate with different quiz and test formats.

Electronic Portfolios

Electronic portfolios (also called e-folios, e-portfolios, or digital portfolios) are a collection of electronic student work with evidence of their learning over time. Portfolios may contain inputted text, electronic files, images, multimedia, student blogs, and hyperlinks. When a portfolio is maintained online, it can be continually updated, added to, enhanced, and pointed to electronically when showing others. Electronic portfolios inherently use multiple literacies and get students thinking about what they have learned, how they know what they know, and how to show it. Building an effective and meaningful portfolio is not simply having students adding their work to a single location. Electronic portfolios are complex and need to be designed purposefully. We describe them briefly here and encourage you to explore them further if you are insipred to use these very powerful tools of student learning. At the end of this section there are links directing you to some very good resources on K–12 student electronic portfolios.

According to Wikipedia, there are three types of electronic portfolios: (1) developmental (e.g., working), (2) reflective (e.g., learning), and (3) representational (e.g., showcase). Developmental portfolios represent a record of what the learner has done over time. Reflective portfolios have similar content to developmental portfolios while adding personal refections on the content. Representational portfolios show work representing achievements toward a goal and are often just certain pieces of work that are selected to best represent progress. It is common for a student electronic portfolio to contain many different types of work and reflect aspects of each type of portfolio—representing learning and growth over time, often in relation to specific projects or assignments, while containing personal reflections and specifically chosen work. Yet, "people often approach electronic portfolios as a multimedia or Web development project and lose sight of the 'showing evidence of learning' component. Reflection, however, plays a critical role in the development of a portfolio. An electronic portfolio is *not* a digital scrapbook" (Baldwin & Stewart, n.d.).

Some schools have adopted electronic portfolios schoolwide and have all students collecting and reflecting on their work. These are great! They are also very expensive if you purchase a system. If you are on a limited budget, there are free ways to have students build their own electronic portfolios. The easiest way to build an electronic portfolio is by using a wiki. Wikis for educational use are free, the owner can give different levels of permission for accessing the wiki (portfolio), and they offer tremendous flexibility in embedding different types of multimedia—text, files, images, blogs, and hyperlinks.

Using Online Project Sites

We hope, by this point, that we have convinced you of the power of incorporating projects into your curriculum. If so, great! That was our intention. Now that we have you hooked, we would like to help you find some online sites that we feel can meet the needs of a technology-rich learning environment such as the one you are developing to enhance literacy.

CCSS Connection

- Translate quantitative or technical information expressed in words in a text into visual form (e.g., a table or chart) and translate information expressed visually or mathematically (e.g., in an equation) into words.
- Use technology, including the Internet, to produce, publish, and update individual or shared writing products, taking advantage of technology's capacity to link to other information and to display information flexibly and dynamically.

There are a variety of online project sites, and they are constantly evolving, adding new materials, developing new directions, and increasing the number of their members. If you do not find something that meets your needs or is a good fit to your curriculum, look on a different site. There is likely to be something on one of them.

Global SchoolNet

Global SchoolNet's (globalschoolnet.org) mission is to "support 21st century learning and improve academic performance through content driven collaboration." Its focus in on engaging project learning exchanges on a worldwide scale that promote literacy and communication skills, among other things. Global SchoolNet lists its available programs and offers ideas about how you can get involved and collaborate. Its range of projects is extensive and should offer a number of appealing choices.

iEARN

iEARN (learn.org) is "the world's largest non-profit global network that enables teachers and youth to use the Internet and other technologies to collaborate on projects that enhance learning and make a difference in the world." Its projects are meaningful to students who see real impact in what they undertake and accomplish. Joining is easy and opens up tremendous resources for project-based learning. All of the projects have been designed by teachers and students, and many illustrate the power of incorporating technology into the learning experience. Additionally, all iEARN projects involve the development of a final product or exhibition for real audiences as an artifact of their learning.

Using the Technology—iEARN

The iEARN homepage is shown in Figure 10.2.

At the time of this writing, there were over 150 projects in iEARN, all designed and facilitated by teachers and students to fit their curriculum and classroom needs and schedules. Projects take

Figure 10.2 iEARN homepage

place in the iEARN Collaboration Center. To participate in one of the currently available projects, participants must select an online project and look at how they can integrate in into their classroom. To get started, go to the iEARN homepage and then go to the "Join/Contact Us" page by clicking that tab at the upper right. The "Join/Contact Us page" is shown in Figure 10.3.

Once you have registered, you will receive information from the iEARN country coordinator in your country. You can search the projects while you are waiting to hear from the

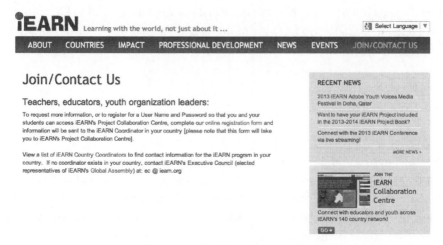

Figure 10.3 iEARN contact page

coordinator or if you are having trouble deciding if there will be something that matches your classroom's needs. Simply have a look at the projects page found at http://media.iearn.org/projects (Figure 10.4).

From there, you can search projects by subject area, grade level, or language. Or view them all for inspiration!

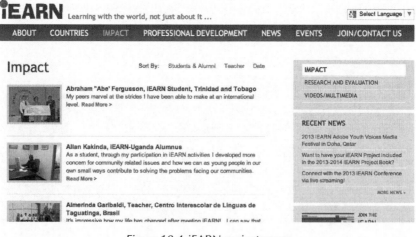

Figure 10.4 iEARN projects page

Education Place

Education Place (eduplace.com) offers a wealth of classroom resources for teachers that are closely tied to their textbook offerings (Education Place is a product of Houghton Mifflin Harcourt). Their project ideas can be used alone or in conjunction with their textbooks. The projects are often closely tied to curriculum standards, making them easier to fit into the demands placed on standards-based-curriculum schools.

TEAMS Educational Resources

TEAMS Educational Resources (teams.lacoe.edu) is produced by the Los Angeles County Office of Education. The webpage offers an excellent list of collaborative Internet projects. Whether you join one of these projects or not, you are sure to be inspired. The projects range from getting connected with experts in the field of study to Earth Day grocery store activities. Many creative ideas abound to inspire you.

An Audience For Learning

Much work has been done looking at the importance of peer review of materials (Falchikov & Goldfinch, 2000). This work reveals that having an audience for the results of learning intensifies the learning for the student (Peck & Dorricott, 1994). While students often publish work that is seen by their local audience including their teacher, classmates, and parents, they seldom publish work that is seen by anyone beyond that. Technology allows students to publish for a much larger audience.

Students are becoming increasingly comfortable with the idea that others will be viewing what they write and post to public sites on the Internet, such as Facebook, tweets and blogs, and YouTube. Does having such a large potential audience for their work intensify what they are learning? In social settings, the research is mixed. In learning settings, the research clearly supports this idea. Having students produce work that will be seen by others outside of their normally small community creates the need to add details, explanations, and supporting evidence and to improve the quality of their writing (Nilson, 2003).

There are many examples of how to have students publish their work. Table 10.3 offers ideas for utilizing just a few. Look at what your students are doing during their personal time on the Internet for additional ideas about audiences for their work.

Table 10.3 Student publication ideas

Publishing Method	Description
Website Publication	Website design has gotten increasingly easier and many students have the skills and desire to build their own. This is a great way to motivate students to publish their work in a personally unique and interesting way. A website provides a framework for publishing work, ideas, and resources. This has the advantage for the author of being able to organize things in relationship to each other for the readers/viewers.
Blogging	Blogs are perhaps the easiest way to get ideas out into the world. They are super easy to create, free, and a great way to increase the audience. A quick Google search for "blogs" will yield many different ones available. The structure of a blog entry is more diary like, in which the author reports on his or her thoughts on a topic or describes a recent experience.

(Continued)

Table 10.3 (Continued)

Publishing Method	Description
Document Sharing	Most likely, Google is the most ubiquitous tool used in your classroom for searching, document sharing, and email. Google has resources for the sharing of student work in Google Groups, Google +, and Google Docs. You can share docs through other sites such as DocStoc and Scribd. A shared document can be just available for reading or set up so others can edit or comment on it. Coauthoring is a common use of these tools. Google Docs allows for the co-creation of documents in real time. Google Groups and Google + facilitate the sharing of materials and the continued collaboration on them.
Slide Show	Slide shows give students a chance to summarize their learning, share what they have learned with others, and expose their thinking. Many teachers have students create slideshows of their work, and publishing can expand the audience for this student work. Zoho Show is a great place to publish slideshows; other great sites are Empressr and SlideShare. The multimedia format of a slide show can garner a greater audience than can a Word document. Presentations posted on Zoho Show can be shared or made public through embedding a link in a blog or website.
Video Presentation	A video presentation demands more creativity and willingness to go on camera than a slideshow presentation. Web 2.0 toolsPhoto Show, Jaycut, Movie Masher, and Motion Box—make the editing and creation of video presentations an easy alternative to "Death by PowerPoint." The video presentations can be shared on blogs, websites, and YouTube.
Magazine Article	If you have students interested in projects involving newsletters or magazine creation, you need to have a look at Yudu and Issuu. Both webspaces will allow your students to turn their static text into powerful online documents rich with audience-grabbing visuals—animations, video, audio, and interactivity. The interactivity helps focus students on the audience/readers' experience in a whole new way. What will they experience? How do I shape their experience? What options do I, as an author, give the reader?
Local Media	Often your local media outlets (television stations, newspapers, town magazine) have opportunities for students to offer their work for publication. Check with the education department of the media group or put in a call to the editor. Students are often very motivated by working on things in their community that they believe are meaningful. Knowing that they may have an audience of hundreds or even thousands of other people in their local area is often just the push they need to be more prolific and improve the quality of their communication.

CCSS Connection

- Synthesize information from a range of sources (e.g., texts, experiments, simulations) into a coherent understanding of a process, phenomenon, or concept, resolving conflicting information when possible.

Summary

Classroom projects have been used for a long time—from the years of solar system dioramas in shoeboxes to dressing up like your favorite character in the story and acting out a scene from a book. The advent of technology in the 21st-century classroom and access to technology at home have changed the nature and scope of potential projects. What has become apparent is the vast opportunity for exploration that students have available to them, as well as the way in which you, their exploration guide, can facilitate their learning through the effective use of existing technologies.

Consider projects that have students researching, collecting data, collaborating, being mentored, going on expeditions, and participating in local, national, and global events. Use online project sites as starting points in the exploration of what is possible. Have students experience the power of producing for an audience to enhance their delivery as well as their motivation to succeed.

While projects may not be the only way to incorporate multi-literacy learning into your classroom they can go a long way toward that end. It is important to keep in mind that each project can offer something accessible to some of your students and utilizing a variety of project ideas is likely to reach them all. The consideration of multimodal learners in education is not a new idea, but one that can now be fully realized with technology.

11   Environments

Spending Time in Their Real World

Students Learning from Other Students

Since the 1960s with the translation of the work of Vygotsky (1962), our understanding of the social nature of learning has grown considerably. The general theory of social learning suggests that students can learn by observing others, imitating others, or modeling their own behavior after the behavior of others around them. The observation of others offers students the opportunity to learn from the behaviors of others and adopt them. If students see a behavior that is successful, they are likely to repeat it themselves. What does it take for students to learn from others? Bandura (1986) wrote about four keys to observational learning, listed here and shown in Figure 11.1:

1. Attention—simply, in order to learn, you need to be paying attention.
2. Retention—to be able to imitate a behavior, you must remember what it was.
3. Reproduction—if you managed to pay attention and remember, you can now employ "practice-makes-perfect" by repeating the behavior until you get it right.
4. Motivation—to continue the behavior, you must be sufficiently motivated—through reward or punishment, especially intrinsic rewards such as interest or curiosity.

Building opportunities for social learning will enhance your students' ability to grasp literacy concepts and learn through them. In addition, increasing your students' experience in social interactions supports the building of their social networks and development of the skills considered critical for future success.

There are many avenues to take that may enhance students' interaction with other students and with it their opportunities to learn from each others' behaviors. From a technological perspective, the collaborative web offers many such opportunities. Students who blog regularly have been shown to have improved writing fluency and lexical complexity (Fellner & Apple, 2006), enhanced collaborative skills (Richardson, 2009), and higher levels of motivation for learning (Downes, 2005).

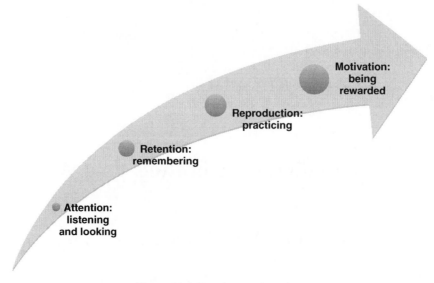

Figure 11.1 Four keys to learning

In this chapter we explore students collaborating virtually with others through a rich technology-enhanced learning environment.

- Virtual Collaborations: Wikis, Blogs, Podcasts, Vodcasts, Modcasts, Cloud Computing, and Gaming
- Social Networks: Building Connections Through Literacy
- Sharing Ideas

Virtual Collaborations

Collaboration is a key component of learning and widely recognized as a critical 21st-century skill. While there are opportunities to get students in classrooms working together, there are far greater opportunities when we look beyond the classroom. Today, utilizing "collaborationware," a student can work with other students to create knowledge on a wiki; share thoughts back and forth using VOIP technologies; publish in blog, podcast, modcast (podcast sent from a mobile phone), or vodcast (video podcast, usually from a smart phone) form; write documents; and share source materials and resources with RSS feeds and tag-sharing sites. These tools are easily learned and yield easily developed collaborations.

Wikis

Wikis, as discussed earlier, are collaborative webspaces for the sharing and development of information and ideas. They are easily created and simple websites that are peer reviewed, group authored, trackable, historical, adaptable, and free. Student contributions to wikis are there for all members to see and review. Having a public audience often enhances the students' desire to produce work of high quality and significance (Fountain, 2005). Other members of the group can add to the wiki as necessary, building on what is already there, editing what has been written, and/or adding new material. Wikis may be used in a variety of settings and topics and lead to knowledge building over time.

CCSS Connection

- Use technology, including the Internet, to produce, publish, and update individual or shared writing products, taking advantage of technology's capacity to link to other information and to display information flexibly and dynamically.

Wikis for Collaboration

Wikis provide opportunities for . . .

- Knowledge building
- Progressive problem solving
- Combining, synthesizing, and evaluating definitions and terminology
- Critically reading and responding to others' work in a constructive and public way
- Learning to add quality and complexity to information

While being . . .

- Democratic
- Real time
- Text based (with embedding capabilities)
- Constructive
- Public

Using the Technology—Wiki (Wikispaces)

There are many wikis to choose from. Here, we use Wikispaces (wikispaces.com) to illustrate how to set up your own wiki. We have used many different ones and find many of the functions and features very similar. We suggest having a look at a few and deciding for yourself what seems to best fit your style and what you see in Figure 11.2.

To get started, click on the green "I'm a Teacher" button. Clicking this will take you to a page containing lots of information about the wiki process. You can jump right in by clicking on the green "Sign Up and Start Your Wiki" button or scroll down the page and look at the tutorials on setting up and working in your wiki.

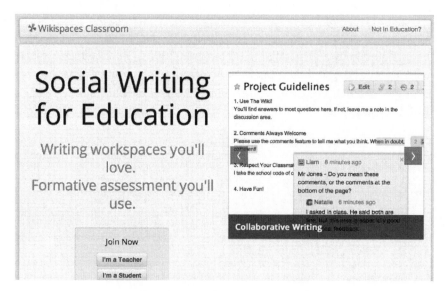

Figure 11.2 Wikispaces main page

Once you have seen enough and feel ready to start building your wiki, sign up or sign in. Creating an account is easy and free; you just need an email address where information will be sent. When you log into your wiki account, you will see a list of the wikis you have created. To create a new wiki, click on the "Create Wiki" button. You will have to give it a name and let Wikispaces know what you intend to use your wiki for.

What your new wiki will look like is shown in Figure 11.3.

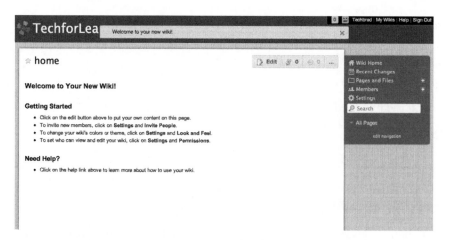

Figure 11.3 Sample of a wiki

Editing your wiki is easy because it uses a "WYSIWYG" editor (What You See Is What You Get) that is very similar to working on a Word document or in Google Docs. Click on the different tutorials to learn about all the different things that can be changed on your wiki. Once you have begun to develop your new wiki, you may want to invite others to be members. Making people members allows them to edit and share materials on the wiki as well. When you make them a member you will need to determine the level of editing permission to give them. Set up a wiki page for a unit and give each student a wiki page. Students can see each other's work and make comments at the bottom of the page. Some pages can be created for posting general resources or other information that is valuable to everyone. If you are concerned that students may edit each other's pages without permission, give each student his or her own wiki with "read only" privileges to the class.

We have seen some very effective uses of wikis with teams. For example, in a biology class, teams were assigned to create a wiki about one of the body's systems. Each wiki began with a template provided by the teacher that included the following elements:

1. Description (must be paraphrased based on at least three sources that are also referenced)
2. How this system works (must include original labeled diagrams or animation and three good resources)
3. How this system interacts with the other systems (paraphrased description by system with at least two resources for each system)
4. How to keep this system healthy (at least five behaviors students can do)
5. Potential problems and treatments
6. Key points to remember (five to eight key points from numbers 1–5)

Blogs

Blogs also offer students a chance to express themselves and collaborate with others. Blogs, coined from the term "web logs," can give students a chance to test out their ideas in writing and offer them up for public review. As the Massachusetts state standards put it, "Read to understand and write to be understood." Blogs can be used as reflective writing journals, for knowledge management, assessment, dialogue as part of group work, as components of e-portfolios, and/ or to share materials. As part of improving their professional practice, teachers can use blogs to share content with the class, network, offer instructional tips for students, mark class milestones for parents, and for knowledge management (logging what you know).

CCSS Connection

- Write informative/explanatory texts, including the narration of historical events, scientific procedures/ experiments, or technical processes.

Blogs for Collaboration

Blogs provide opportunities for . . .

- Collaboration on complex tasks through idea sharing
- Improvement of written communication skills
- Reflection on experiences
- Easy self-publication

While being . . .

- A showcase of thought over time
- Familiar web format
- Public
- Accepting of responses/comments
- Free

When a blog entry is made public, there is a comment or response space given to the reader. The public access to what is written, and to the ideas shared within, sets up a venue for an exchange between the author and his or her audience. This exchange can provide feedback to the authors on how clearly they were able to express their thoughts and can build relationships with people interested in their ideas.

Podcasts, Vodcasts, and Modcasts

Podcasts are audio publications similar to homemade radio that are published to the Internet. Vodcasts, podcasts' video equivalent, have become increasingly common, as have modcasts (podcasting from your mobile device). The essence of a podcast is creating content for an audience that wants to listen. Listeners have the ultimate control—listening when they want, where they want, and how they want. Listeners can choose to listen utilizing their mobile device and often listen while performing other activities. Podcasts take the notion of "anywhere, anytime learning" and literally put it into the hands of students.

CCSS Connection

- Use technology, including the Internet, to produce and publish writing and present the relationships between information and ideas clearly and efficiently.

The collaborative nature of podcasts comes from the exchange of information and ideas between community members. Produced work that is listened to can be responded to either in blog or podcast format. The continued exchange of ideas not only engages the learner in the content but also encourages the expansion of literacy skills. Varying the delivery techniques of the message can also benefit different learning styles in the classroom. Learners with strong auditory learning styles may have a difficult time reading blogs and responding while they may thrive in the auditory environment of podcasts. In this way, technology becomes a powerful tool in the delivery of appropriate teaching and learning strategies. Podcasts also allow access to information in a nonlinear fashion. Podcast users can access information in the podcast at any point they feel is necessary and in so doing increase their control over their learning. The producers of podcasts have the potential of a real audience that follows their thinking so they are motivated to make them engaging.

Cloud Computing

No matter what platform you or your school utilizes, you most likely use a word processing software program that may or may not include other features like spreadsheets, presentations, or desktop functionality. It is also nearly certain that each of the machines has the software loaded onto it directly, allowing it to function independently. When changes to software occur, each machine must be updated by physically inserting the new software CD/DVD and loading it. This is a time-consuming and potentially problematic process. If you don't believe us, go ask someone in the computer support department. They will be happy to share horror stories about the last installation update, and to prevent such problems they often tightly control what gets installed.

Cloud computing (Figure 11.4) represents a paradigm shift in how we think about computers and their relationship to information. Cloud computing is any Internet-based tool that acts as a means to store and later access information on a remote server rather than a local computer; it can be manipulated even though nothing is on your personal computer. Computers utilizing this tool can be much simpler, needing very little internal memory or processing speed but relying instead on a robust Internet connection.

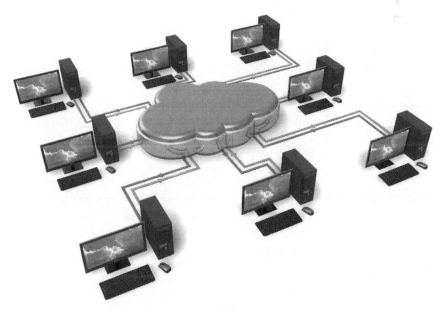

Figure 11.4 Cloud computing

For our purposes here, we discuss the Google line of products and their potential applications for the cloud. Google currently offers the largest array of cloud-based products and services, most of which are free. Within the Google line of products are a word processor, spreadsheet program, and presentation software, all part of Google Docs and all free. Documents can be shared, collectively worked on, grouped together, and edited from any machine with an Internet connection. These represent significant advantages to traditional systems but also pose a few risks.

The advantages are that students' work is housed online, alleviating the issues with saving, losing, and locating work. Also, students can work collaboratively on assignments either synchronously or asynchronously. Students working on shared documents can leave each other notes and feedback, set up times to talk through Google Chat, and organize their work using a shared calendar. The major downside is that nothing happens without Internet access. Without access to the Internet, students cannot access their work, share their documents, read what has been done by others, or anything else. While this is a major consideration, the cost savings from moving away from purchasing software and associated updates may be enough to offset the additional costs of improving school and home access to the Internet.

Cloud computing supports multi-literacy use and development through a variety of features. First, because the cloud houses the applications to be used, it offers the potential for all students to access a large array of different software applications from whatever location they find themselves. Second, by its very nature, the cloud is dynamic and ever changing. This helps create a state of opportunity for learners of different types as they explore and begin to house their artifacts within the cloud. Third, since the support for multi-literacy in schools may be challenging, support from within the cloud in the form of resources, information, and experts is always there from any connected digital device.

Gaming—Beyond Games as Perks

Propelled to prominence by Sawyer and Rejeski's launching of the Serious Games movement, utilization of video games and simulations to teach has emerged as a leading force in educational game design (Mayo, 2009). Serious games are those games designed to achieve non-entertainment goals, including education of the learner. Learner success in emerging serious game environments requires 21st-century skills, including systems thinking, problem solving, information tracking, collaboration, information sharing, leadership, and teamwork (Mayo, 2009). Today, there exist numerous education-focused gaming environments covering a wide variety of subject areas.

New gaming and simulation environments also rely heavily on social engagement. Learners interact with peers, develop in-world characters, and take on roles that differ from what they have in the "real world." Second Life (secondlife.com) was the first massively utilized immersive world. While it was not designed with educational purposes in mind, much work has been done to develop in-world educational opportunities for its members. NOAA, for instance, has developed a very rich and detailed "island" where Second Life members can ride a Hurricane Hunter C130 Aircraft (Figure 11.5) into the eye of a hurricane or ride a weather balloon into the upper layers of our atmosphere. For those looking to explore different cultures, try a visit to the Apollo Theater in Harlem in New York City (Figure 11.6).

Figure 11.5 Hurricane Hunter C130 aircraft

Figure 11.6 Apollo Theater

While some schools have begun to adopt games and simulations into their curriculum, their utilization is overwhelmingly informal and in non-educational settings. In this way, gaming continues to be primarily a social and recreational pursuit by users (Ito et al., 2009). The next chapter looks at how virtual worlds, simulations, and serious games can be utilized to promote learning and literacy.

Social Networks—Building Connections Through Literacy

Who is not familiar with Facebook? Most likely, you have your own Facebook page and have updated your profile recently. Chances are that your students have too. Social network spaces such as Facebook have developed into some of the most trafficked Internet sites, receiving more than a million hits daily and boasting membership of over 300 million and growing.

Figure 11.7 Facebook schools page

Facebook is not the only social network site on the Internet, although as of this writing, it is the most popular. Other sites include those similar to Facebook such as MySpace, Ning, and Habbo, as well as spaces connecting people with similar interests such as Flickster and the World of Warcraft Forum Community. The National School Boards Association (NSBA) reports nearly 60% of those students regularly using social networking sites talk about educational topics in their online space and 50% talk specifically about their current schoolwork and assignments (NSBA, 2007)—promoting interaction between members of the virtual community around school-related activities from the physical world.

Many schools have developed their own Facebook pages (Figure 11.7) where they list school events, publish school calendars, link to student work, post announcements, and more. These spaces are private, requiring as invitation to join. They have become increasingly popular alternatives to developing expensive school websites. Within schools, classroom teachers are utilizing social networking spaces as a way to share class notes and general classroom information while providing opportunities for students to interact by sharing project ideas or study materials or by providing peer tutoring, and homework help. Other spaces have connected classrooms from different parts of the world to collaborate and share.

Social Network Collaborative Ideas

- Language Students—Spanish learners in the United States connecting with English learners in Spain for conversations and learning about each other's cultures
- Science Concepts—Students testing science concepts combining data with another school to compare results and build datasets for analysis
- History Connections—Partnering with a school in a region of the United States or world where the historical events took place or where there are related current events
- Topic Clubs—Clubs where students connect and share with other like-minded students on shared interests such as science, engineering, geology, anime, or particular authors
- Student and Parent Writing Groups—A space for students and parents to collaborate in writing about topics of local interest, careers, or current events

- Art E-Folios—Development of online portfolios for students to share and exhibit their work while engaging in conversations with others
- Connected Classrooms—Linking classrooms across the hall or across the world to share ideas, experiences, and connections

Literary Groups

Many gathering places have sprung up on the Internet where like-minded literary fans can meet and share their passions for words, characters, books, or authors. Bringing one's love for literature into the open within a supportive community helps to enhance people's sense of belonging in a group where there are others like them. Adult book clubs and reading groups have been commonplace for years. Increasingly, reading groups (literature circles, literature discussion groups) are becoming popular in K–12 classrooms (Daniels, 1994). These literacy groups are usually small groups of three to five students who gather to discuss a book they are reading or just finished reading. The teacher may offer guiding questions, or students may direct the discussion.

Student-guided literary groups often rely on questions generated from student reading journals kept while reading from the text or from discussion topics generated by the group itself. There is no right way to organize a literary group. Literary circles take different shapes in different classrooms and are different on different days. What is most important is that true engagement occurs between the students and the material.

Traditionally, student literature groups have been conducted face to face in the classroom, and their membership has been limited by the classroom size. Having the ability to connect with others outside of the classroom, either in traditional ways such as buddy classes or less traditional ways such as connecting with others virtually, expands our community of learners and so expands our exposure to other like-minded people. Virtual connections, enabled by the Internet, allow students to find others working on and discussing the same topics or stories. By expanding their community, they expose themselves to new ideas and new ways of thinking. We can't overlook those connections, as shown in the cartoon in Figure 11.8.

Discussion is a critical component of any literary group, regardless of size or location, and can be facilitated in a variety of ways. The classroom teacher can be directly involved with the group, asking the questions and setting the direction of the discussion; can be directly involved as a group member; can be an outside observer; or can roam the room while the students facilitate their own groups. In a virtual environment, the teacher can acquire transcripts of the discussion, listen in, lurk, or facilitate.

Some of our favorite project ideas to enhance student engagement in reading and offer opportunities for students to collaborative within their literary circles include the following:

- Character Timeline—Develop a timeline of the major events in a chosen character's life. A hyperlinked document, webspace, or wiki can act as the reading portfolio.
- Alternate Ending—Write a different ending that ties to events in the reading and offers a plausible end, with explanations as to why and how it was chosen.

Figure 11.8 Cartoon about technology in schools

- Character Advice—Being able to take the concerned observer role allows students to think about the characters' actions and offer advice as to how they could have done things differently. Offering these comments to the group opens discussion about actions and consequences.

- Artistic Representation—Students inclined to draw, paint, sing, or act may like to represent a perspective, response, feeling, or other tie to the reading through artistic representation.

- Book Review—A newspaper-style book review gives students a chance to look critically at a book for its value to others and brings to their attention the world of book reviews.

- Character Blog—Students may want to blog about things happening in the book or in a particular character's life. Blogs may be fictional, written from the character's perspective or written about the character from an outside perspective.

- Newscast—A "Reporting Live From the Scene" newscast offers students a chance to collaborate to produce a response to the material in a fun and creative way.

Sharing with YouTube/Teacher Tube

Reading aloud is a powerful way to enhance reading and writing proficiency. Reading aloud and having the chance to view yourself doing so are even more powerful, allowing for self-correction. Have your students read poetry, stories, or text aloud and record them with a camera or microphone directly on the computer or uploaded from a separate device. The recordings do not need to be in high definition or done to the highest professional standards. Rather, recordings done with small and inexpensive hand-held video cameras work great, as do those done with cell phones and from the video camera built into computers.

Editing of the video, when necessary, has become easier than ever with online editing software that allows the user to upload the video and edit it online—eliminating the need to have expensive software. A quick search for "free online video editing" should yield the needed results. Once edited, if necessary, load the video onto YouTube or use Teacher Tube to address privacy issues. Although both are free, you will need to have an account for either of these to add videos.

Whatever the medium, allow students to view the product and redo it as many times as they want. Seeing themselves as they would see someone else can accelerate the development of their communication skills and help students develop self-critique skills that will serve them in any learning situation.

Summary

Social learning is at the center of student learning. Students learn by observing others, imitating others, or modeling their own behavior after the behavior of others around them. Utilizing available technology can help to enhance these types of social interactions. Build social learning opportunities into you lesson plans to help engage your students in meaningful learning experiences. Wikis are a great way to offer collaborative learning opportunities, blogs for offering students the opportunity to share their work with others in a public forum, and podcasts, vodcasts, and modcasts bring an engaging learning opportunity of for students to share with others in a public setting.

Students are likely very comfortable with social networks. Social networks can be leveraged to promote collaborative learning for students in a variety of classes and school groups. Social media also allows students to interact with piers across the world to discuss and share meaningful experiences and interests. Specialty online groups expand the learning opportunities and enhance the social nature of the learning. When you think about learning environments, think about what students are choosing to participate in outside of school. These environments are social and engaging. Leverage them to do both in your classroom.

Developing a Personal Learning Network

The effect of technology on students' access to knowledge is determined by the pedagogical knowledge and skill of teachers. Technology enables teachers with well-developed working theories of student learning to extend the reach and power of those theories; in the absence of these powerful theories, technology enables mediocrity.

—Coppola, 2004, p. xii

Introduction

Keeping up with the daily demands of being a teacher—the lectures, activities, projects, homework, behavior issues, parents, meetings, and more—can make learning new technologies a daunting task. It is, however, a critical one. Today's students are exposed to and adopting new technologies at an ever-increasing rate, and finding ways to incorporate them into the classroom will enhance students' interest in the subjects and the knowledge acquisition process. It would seem odd if banks, hospitals, industry, or finance used less technology or refused to adopt technologies that would enhance their ability to function. This holds true for education as well. We simply cannot refuse to use effective learning technologies that our students are already using outside of school.

While businesses look to adopt emerging technologies, they also struggle with the same issues as do teachers in their classrooms. Businesses must understand the technologies and how they might be useful, find ways to stay competitive, heed the demands of their customers, offer enhanced services, and look for ways that technology may enhance their current practices. To do these things, businesses do not work alone. They partner with experts, look at what their competitors are doing, and listen to their customers to help shape their technology adoption. Businesses must also stay true to their original business plan or mission statement, just as Coppola (2004) reminds us that technology is most useful for those teachers with "well developed working theories of student learning" (p. xii). Technology adoption in the classroom is less beneficial without a sound pedagogical understanding of how it is going to be utilized and an understanding of how others have successfully used the technology and its impact on our clients, the students.

The Pew Internet & American Life Project (Levin & Arafeh, 2002) found that students of all ages use multiple technologies extensively and that as their age increases so do the amount of their use and the diversity of technologies they employ. In this study, students were very positive about utilizing technology, mainly the Internet, to complete school assignments from home. Their perceptions of technology use in the classroom were not nearly as positive and depended on a few factors. First, students believed their teachers had insufficient knowledge. Second, they reported having a disappointing level of quality access and that pervasive filtering systems (blockers and filters) kept them from accessing critical information. Third, while there were expectations of positive and engaging use of the Internet when assigned by their teachers, they felt the assignments were often of poor quality.

Having been teachers ourselves, we both point first to teachers as the most critical component of any successful classroom. The introduction of technology and its effective utilization are no different. Research clearly indicates that the single most important factor in the effective use of technology is the quality of the teacher's knowledge of effective technology uses in instruction (Coppola, 2004). So, the question is, "How can teachers effectively learn to utilize technology for instruction?" The rest of this chapter explores this question and suggests you start to build your personal learning network (PLN; Tobin, 1998) to meet this need because a PLN about technology will help you develop your skills, support your troubleshooting, and keep you tuned in to effective uses of technology.

Steps to Building Your PLN

First, ask yourself where you are on the social technographics ladder (Baumbach, 2009) (See Figure 12.1.)

Don't be discouraged if you are at the bottom now. In a short time, you will find yourself moving up the technology ladder. If you are a spectator in some ways, a joiner in others, and a creator in others, that is terrific. Even if you are not yet involved beyond spectating, you can use the following suggestions to help build your PLN and begin to master technologies that can enhance learning and literacy development in your classroom.

Building a PLN is, first and foremost, an active process. You are the one who will benefit, and so it is your responsibility to build your network and fill it with the things you need to be successful. Building a successful and beneficial PLN consists of five steps:

Step 1—Join some social networks.
Step 2—Get connected.
Step 3—Grow your voice online.
Step 4—Build your knowledge through online activity.
Step 5—Develop relationships.

Any of these steps, taken individually, will go a long way in enhancing your ability to effectively incorporate technology in your classroom and improve literacy, but taken together, they offer you a unique opportunity to incorporate your personal growth, new understanding, and new skills into a sound pedagogy for learning through multi-literacies. It is important to remember that we increase our capacity when we work together rather than working in isolation. The attributes of a PLN bring together the strengths of the community to develop stronger professionals. Successful

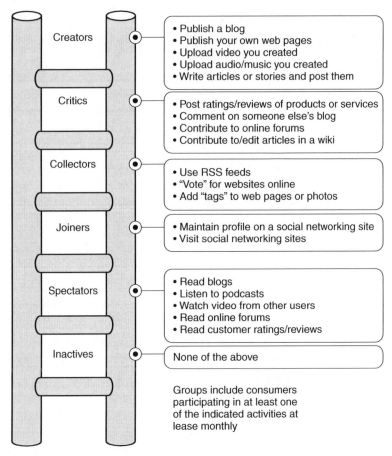

Creators
- Publish a blog
- Publish your own web pages
- Upload video you created
- Upload audio/music you created
- Write articles or stories and post them

Critics
- Post ratings/reviews of products or services
- Comment on someone else's blog
- Contribute to online forums
- Contribute to/edit articles in a wiki

Collectors
- Use RSS feeds
- "Vote" for websites online
- Add "tags" to web pages or photos

Joiners
- Maintain profile on a social networking site
- Visit social networking sites

Spectators
- Read blogs
- Listen to podcasts
- Watch video from other users
- Read online forums
- Read customer ratings/reviews

Inactives
None of the above

Groups include consumers participating in at least one of the indicated activities at lease monthly

Figure 12.1 Social technographics ladder

PLNs combine supportive and shared leadership, collective creativity, shared values and practices, supportive conditions, people, and shared personal practice.

Step 1: Joining Social Networks

The first step in building your PLN is to become part of the rapidly growing educational technology community. We see two worthwhile ways of spending your time doing this: through social networking and learning from online resources. There are many social networks and online networks available today, and they all have one thing in common: They bring people together.

Social Networking

Everyone has heard of Facebook. Facebook users share information about themselves with others, join groups, collaborate, solve problems, share knowledge, gain insights, share photos, and can do just about anything you could imagine that involves communication. Facebook also offers users the opportunity to search for groups focused on specific issues. You might want to search for teachers using technology groups or using technology in creative ways. Facebook is by no means the only or best social network site out there. Search Ning for some excellent social networks, or try YouTube and iEARN. There are many social network sites, and each offers different things to different groups of people.

Ning is a do-it-yourself social network webspace that provides its users the opportunity to create their own social network or search and join others. You will find many groups focused on education and on the incorporation of technology such as Classroom 2.0, the Global Education Collaborative, NextGen Teachers, and Professional Development. While Facebook and Ning are not the only social networks you may want to explore and join, they do offer a nice introduction into what social networking spaces can offer and allow you to start to build your PLN.

Learning from Resources

If you are struggling with how to learn new technologies you are not alone. To help assist you, a number of teacher technology "help" websites have emerged. Most offer valuable guidelines and numerous links to additional resources. As mentioned earlier, blogs and podcasts are also excellent sources for new information and learning; podcasts have the additional convenience of being portable and can be listened to on your personal audio player anywhere you happen to be. Don't forget to check YouTube for "how-to" videos.

Free Technology For Teachers is a blog written for teachers who want to expand their understanding and use of technology in their classroom (www.4teachers.org). It is written by a Google Certified Teacher, links to multiple resources, and offers a great variety of topics for beginners to seasoned technology users. Google Certified Teachers are educators who have successfully completed Google Teacher Academy, a free professional development experience designed to help primary and secondary educators from around the globe get the most from innovative technologies (www.google.com/edu/programs/google-teacher-academy). You can subscribe and receive updates and even follow the blogger on Twitter. What is that? You don't use Twitter? Well, now seems like as good a time as any to start! Not sure how to get a Twitter account? Ask your students. One of them is likely a regular tweeter. While *Free Technology For Teachers* is an excellent resource, there are others. A quick search on Google using "teacher resources for technology use" yielded over 170 million results with five very useful ones on the first page:

- Use of Technology in Teaching and Learning—www.ed.gov/oii-news/use-technology-teaching-and-learning
- 4Teachers—www.4teachers.org
- Ed Tech Teacher—http://edtechteacher.org
- Center of Teaching Excellence—www.smu.edu/Provost/CTE/Resources/Technology
- PBS Teachers—www.pbs.org/teachers

PBS Teachers was one of the websites that appeared on the first page of our search (www.pbs.org/teachers). PBS Teachers is organized by the student/teacher grade level and allows users free access to content specific for Pre-K, K–2, 3–5, 6–8, and 9–12 grades.

Another way to help build your own literacy in educational technology is to form a tech group at your school. Similar to how you might develop a group with your students, get fellow teachers to list what technologies they feel they could teach and then leverage them as experts for that particular technology. Members of the tech group may want to give weekly presentations that spotlight a particular technology and how they are implementing it in their classroom to help facilitate learning. To make this a more valuable experience for the members, be sure to identify the underlying pedagogy and give specific examples of how it has been used successfully in the past, with accompanying printed material for others to reference when necessary.

Step 2: Getting Connected

Getting connected is easier and more important than ever. A great deal is happening out there in the world, and fortunately, it is easier than ever to keep up with it all. RSS (short for **R**eal **S**imple **S**yndication) allows you to subscribe to news sources, blogs, podcasts, and the like and have that material sent directly to the location of your choosing, including your email in-box or mobile device. RSS readers allow you to gather all of your RSS feeds into one place and offer you tools to better access the information you are looking for through search features, keywords, topics, tagging, and other connections.

Like many tools on the Internet, there are many RSS readers available for free, and a quick search on Google or Bing should yield many choices. For starters, try Google Reader or Netvibes. Both are simple to use and offer good tutorials that will explain the process and walk you through step by step how to get set up. You may also want to subscribe to a podcast through iTunes. iTunes is not just for Macintosh computer users, and it is free. Once you have iTunes on your computer, browse the podcasts and search for those that are most interesting and important to you. There are many to choose from to get and stay connected.

In addition to podcasts, RSS feeds are available for many blogs as well. Utilizing RSS technology can bring you into contact on a regular basis with some of the most interesting and thoughtful people in education today. Instead of having to go to a site to get updates, the updates come to or are "fed" to you so you are in the loop all the time, getting the most up-to-date information.

In 2006, the Online Education Database (OEDb; www.oedb.org) released its "Top 100 Education Blogs" picks. At that time OEDb indicated that Edublogs.com hosted over 30,000 blogs alone and that there were likely to be thousands of other blogs with an educational focus. With such a wealth of resources freely available online through blogs, it is easy to get connected with others in the educational community.

Step 3: Growing Your Voice Online—Blog, Modcast, Vodcast, and Tweet on Twitter

Once you have gotten connected and established yourself as a regular on blogs sites and with podcasts, it is the time to get off the sidelines and start writing some of your own. Writing your own material might include blogging, modcasting (blogging/podcasting from your mobile device), vodcasting (creating video podcasts from your mobile device), and tweeting (using Twitter). While you might not feel you have too much to say at first, reading what others are writing and then giving and getting feedback can help prepare you. Look for an area that you feel passionate about and start there. It is important to remember that most people with established blogs and many followers once felt similarly to how you feel now. Whether you have a passion for improving early readers' literacy or helping emerging storytellers, it is likely you have something to contribute to the dialogue occurring online.

An easier way to start might be to "tweet" about your educational experiences. "Tweets" are what Twitter users post as a way of communicating with others within their community. Each text-based post containing up to 140 characters gets delivered to subscribers and can have embedded links to others' tweets, pictures, or other online information. Additionally, some very interesting thought leaders tweet, and you can join their tweet network and hear what they have to say. Often the thoughts of others spur thoughts of your own.

Using the Technology—Twitter

So you think you want to tweet, be a Twitter user, and tweet to your followers. Well, the first thing you need is a Twitter account. They are free and only take a minute of two to create. First go to Twitter.com and begin by entering your name, email, and a password into the sign-up box on the right. Once you have completed the signing-up process, you will have a homepage that shows all of the Twitter feeds you are following and who is following you. Your homepage will look similar to Figure 12.2.

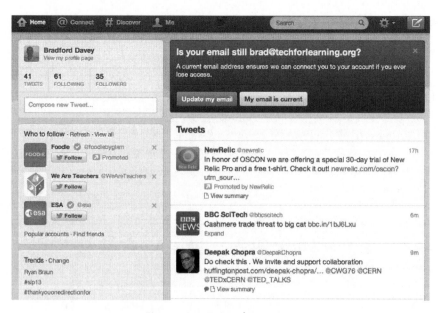

Figure 12.2 Twitter homepage

To write a new tweet, simply click the feather pen blue box at the upper right or write it in the compose box directly below your name in the "Compose New Tweet . . ." box. Remember, a tweet must be no longer than 140 characters, including spaces. This can be a fun challenge, and frequent tweeters get very good at meeting this space limitation. There are also other features to creating tweets that are helpful. Hashtags are perhaps the most important. A hashtag (the "#" symbol embedded in a tweet) is used to mark a keyword or topic in a tweet. It is a way to categorize messages. For example, let's say you want your students to tweet about a project they are working on, and to help organize their tweets, you ask them to the use the hashtag "#MRSMITH." Going forward, every tweet that has this hashtag in it will be organized together, allowing everyone to see what everyone else is tweeting about the project. There are many hashtag help sites that can offer advice and directions for using them that are much more detailed than we have included here.

You can search using the search box at the top of the page. There are tweets on just about everything out there. Finding just what you are looking for may be difficult because of the volume, but some careful searches may reveal just what you want. It is often helpful to see who others are following. Read a few of their tweets and see what they are writing about. Perhaps they are writing about things that interest you. Be aware that, once you are on Twitter, your students may find you. You may want this and, if so, great. Just be mindful of what you tweet about.

Step 4: Building Your Knowledge—Attend a Webinar and Online Conference (or Two)

Many educational organizations offer online free webinars as part of educational series throughout the year. You should first look at the educational organizations that you have become part of either through your current educational work or from the first steps in building your PLN. It is likely that one of the professional organizations that you currently belong to offers an annual or regional conference. It is increasingly common for these same organizations to offer some or all of their conferences online. For example, FETC, the Florida Educational and Technology Conference, has begun to simulcast some conference sessions and make others available online for those unable to physically attend. Professional journals are another great source for increasingly more virtual content aimed at educational audiences.

Examples of journals and organizations that offer webinars are T.H.E. Journal (Technology Horizons in Education) and the International Society for Technology in Education (ISTE). The webinars from T.H.E. Journal cover a wide range of subject matter focused on education. They are free and you can subscribe to them through email; the embedded link allows you to click and go. ISTE webinars are more content specific while staying focused on educational technology integration and utilization. ISTE webinars are fee based, costing around $50 for members, and their announcements arrive in your email. It is important to keep in mind that there are many educational organizations out there that offer their own unique perspectives on educational pursuits. So you may need to explore them for a while until you find one that offers you just what you need in a way that you find appealing and beneficial. Webinars are a great way to stay up to date and be informed about what is happening.

There are also online conferences held in virtual worlds and many are free. You are likely to begin to hear about them as soon as you immerse yourself in the blogosphere and subscribe to more podcasts. Online conferences are great because there is no travel necessary, you can come and go as necessary, listen in when you have time, preview the schedule and pick and choose what you like, and listen to recorded sessions that you missed. You may want to try Learning 2.008 (learning2cn.ning.com), K12Online (http://k12online.us), the Future of Learning in a Networked World (http://flnw.wikispaces.com), or ones held in Second Life. While it may take some getting used to, being a virtual conference or webinar participant allows you to take advantage of educational opportunities and interact with other educators whom you might never encounter otherwise.

Step 5: Developing Relationships and Personal Connections

You must be intentional in bringing all these steps together. Whether they are relationships with other people, information, or technology, they must be continually developed, grown, and nurtured. Don't be afraid to talk to the other people at the online conference you attend, respond to others' blog posts, blog yourself, or form a tech support group at your school. Just get out there and try it. Please remember that if you get stuck, just as your students do sometimes, do what you suggest they do and ask for help. Your world just got a whole lot larger, and someone will be willing and able to help you.

Perhaps the most immediate and important component to learning new technologies as part of your participation in the community is to enlist help from someone who knows more than you. It the case of technology, the answer as to who this might be is likely right in front of you each and every day: It's your students. Your students are digital natives (Prensky, 2001). They have been raised on a steady diet of YouTube, Facebook, Twitter, blogs, games, and the Internet. They are highly adapted people with highly developed beliefs about technology. Digital natives look on technology as their friend. They take it for granted. They are comfortable in a digital world, connected, experiential, immediate, and highly social. They rely on technology, using it to study, work, play, relax, and communicate. You may need to learn to rely on them. They are multi-literate, but may not be using efficient or effective literacy strategies, which you can help them develop while they help you with the nuts and bolts of the technology.

Employing students in your quest to better utilize technology as a teaching tool can take many forms. Simply observing students as they interact with technology might be the first place to start. Digital natives interact differently, think differently, continually support their digital identity, have different levels of digital creativity, and have taken multitasking to a new level. When observing your students, watch how they use the technology to aid in their learning. Give them some freedom to explore and watch as they explore the Internet, searching to find information and gather evidence. It is likely that their search patterns will vary dramatically from what you might expect in how they are structured, or are unstructured, and follow a nonlogical pattern. Their searching is not random or illogical, however. They often have developed a very advanced understanding of how information is connected and can be accessed. Get them to talk about it. An analysis of students' process behaviors illustrated that children are interactive information seekers, preferring to browse rather than plan or employ systematic analytic-based searching strategies (Schacter, Chung, & Dorr, 1998). Notice what they do that works, and where there are gaps or inefficiencies in how they obtain, process, organize, and retain information.

Your students are also likely to have multiple windows open on the computer simultaneously. Most students listen to music while on the computer (80%), often are watching TV while studying (75%), texting (75%), talking on the phone (70%), and/or visiting a site mentioned by someone they are on the phone with (50%; ECAR, 2004). Having multiple windows open and performing multiple tasks simultaneously does not mean they are not on task; rather, it emphasizes their nonlinear approach to learning and how they attach meaning to information. Recent research on multitasking (Moore, 2010; Wallis, 2006) shows that it is not always efficient or effective. Challenge students to consciously focus on one task and complete it. Encourage them to systematically use a variety of strategies to read, write, and produce.

You can use technology to multitask. Start by listening to a podcast on your drive to work. Talk with your students about the literacy skills you notice in this experience—what you are listening to and what you notice about how you comprehend, process, and retain what you hear. Talk about how the podcast is produced. Ask them to talk about what they listen to in this way. There are many free educational podcasts available online that cover a variety of subjects and are often searchable by grade focus and topic. The table below offers a few of our favorites and a quick search with the description of "educational podcasts" will yield a current list.

Podcast	Description
Podcast Alley	Podcast Alley is a podcast portal offering listeners a clearinghouse of available podcasts. Podcasts include education topics, information for educational institutions, or podcasts about education.
Learning in Hand	Listing of educational podcasts and instructions for subscribing, listening, and creating your own
Podcast.com	Huge listing of available educationally focused podcasts. Education podcasts from universities, colleges, students, teachers—everyone who uses podcasting to learn and to teach others
Podbean.com	An educational podcast directory with interesting podcasts about learning from a student perspective
EdTechTalk	Huge educational network run and developed by educators and completely free
NPR	National Public Radio offers a large selection of current topics available for free download and subscription
Grammar Girl	Podcast available for the development of better writers

Students Leading Discussions, Presentations, Demonstrations, and Teaching

The classroom teacher is the key variable in technology integration and effectiveness (Fulton, 1998) and is responsible for opening the classroom to more communication opportunities for all its members. Try to encourage more teacher–student and student–student discussions about technology by sharing authority. Give students the chance to lead discussions about their experiences with the technology they utilize. Students may want to demonstrate their use of gaming to learn, their virtual environments like Teen Second Life, or how they developed their own blogs or podcasts. Make thinking about the use of technology a regular part of your classroom discussions. Reflecting about "how I learned" or "what I learned about learning" is a great way to get students used to doing metacognition (thinking about thinking).

Having students present their experiences creates opportunities for their complex, authentic, and meaningful experiences to become part of the learning in your classroom. As touchstones for conversation, reading, and writing, these presentations connect your students to each other and reinforce that they have something important to communicate. Your students may also form groups around similar interests and experiences. For example, World of Warcraft players might want to form a classroom guild and play together, artists could share collaborative work spaces, musicians might develop a "band" and write music together, or students could form an environmental action group dedicated to identifying a local issue and what they might be able to do to effect change.

Students may also be able and willing to teach fellow students (and you) how to use the technology tools they know. Start by opening a dialogue about technologies that your students use, and then have them rate their level of proficiency with each on a scale of 1–10, from "I don't know anything about it" to "I can teach it." Recognize the students who identify themselves as able to teach a technology as experts, and enlist them to develop a plan to instruct others.

Engaging students in classroom activities and projects does not mean that you need to be an expert in the technology yourself. Don't shy away from different activities because of their level of technological complexity. If you get stuck, be honest with your students and troubleshoot together. Table 12.1 offers some great classroom activities based on proven pedagogy that utilizes technology. Each is designed to give students a chance to collaborate, utilize an expertise or skill, and focus on something they may be interested in, and each provides a meaningful experience.

Key ideas

- Project-based learning can be used as a powerful learning tool in conjunction with 21st-century technologies.
- Students learn by researching, collecting data, collaborating with their peers, being mentored, and exploring.
- There are many online project sites that can help facilitate project-based learning in the classroom.
- Having work reviewed by peers, stakeholders, and other audiences is a powerful learning tool and intensifies learning.

Table 12.1 Sample student activities

Activity	Description
One-Act Play Script	Using a wiki, have students collaboratively write a one-act play. Using the wiki, students work collectively to complete the project and share ideas that shape the outcome.
Public Service Announcement	Build a PSA using any variety of media sources that inform about an issue important to the students.
Animated Story	Students are often writing fictitious stories as part of their English/Language Arts classroom work. Have students animate one of their stories by working with an online animation tool.
Comic Book Hero	Utilizing one of the online comic book writing tools, students share their work with others and offer feedback that is incorporated into additional versions and other stories.
School Newspaper	Whether as a club or part of a class assignment, students lead the development of an online school newspaper.

- Students can publish their ideas for their peers through blogging, document sharing, slide shows, video, writing articles, and local media.
- Group projects work well because students learn from other students when they are in close proximity and have shared goals. Incidental learning goes up because they are paying attention to what is said, retaining what they see and hear to use in the project, copying each other's successful behaviors, and feeling motivated to succeed in front of their peers.
- Keeping up with technology can be a big challenge for any educator—building a personal learning network will help.

Summary

In Section IV we have discussed how reading, writing, speaking, listening, viewing, and producing come together in a multi-literacy environment. After an introduction to multi-literacies, Chapter 10 presented projects and how emerging educational technologies provide opportunities to reach every student in a unique way. Not all students can be reached with any particular learning theory, but using a variety of tools in close support of sound teaching and learning helps ensure all students are met.

In Chapter 11 we looked at how the social nature of learning has grown considerably with the introduction of 21st-century technologies into the classroom, which enable students to reach out to other students, find resources, and have larger audiences for their work. Making their work more public encourages students to produce the best work they can and to ask for help to improve it. Students can pursue individual interests, collaborate with other students in the class or elsewhere, and tap into resources beyond their local community.

In Chapter 12 we suggested you develop your own personal learning network for using technology resources, continue to learn about literacy strategies by experiencing them, and connect with others who have the same interests or have expertise that can help you in your classroom. We also walk you through the development of your PLN, what steps to take for it to be successful, and how to use it to learn and facilitate your continued growth.

References for Section IV

Bandura, A. (1986). *Social foundations of thought and action: A social cognitive theory*. Englewood Cliffs, NJ: Prentice-Hall.

Baldwin, M., & Stewart, N. (n.d.). *Enrichment matters*. www.enrichmentmatters.com

Barron, B. (1998). Doing with understanding: Lessons from research on problem- and project-based learning. *Journal of the Learning Sciences, 7*(3/4), 271—311.

Baumbach, D. J. (2009). Web 2.0 and you. *Knowledge Quest, 37*(4), 12–19.

Boss, S., & Krauss, J. (2007). *Reinventing project based learning: Your field guide to real-world projects in the digital age*. Eugene, OR: International Society for Technology in Education.

Bransford, J. D., Brown, A. L., & Cocking, R. R. (2000). *How people learn: Brain, mind, experience, and school*. Washington, DC: National Research Council.

Cisco Systems. (2008). *Multimodal learning through media: What the research says*. Retrieved February 2010 from http://tinyurl.com/mml9yyo

Coppola, E. M. (2004). *Powering up: Learning to teach well with technology*. New York: Teachers College Press.

Dale, E. (1954). *Audio-visual methods in teaching*. New York: Dryden.

Daniels, H. (1994). *Literature circles: Voice and choice in the student-centered classroom*. Markham: Pembroke Publishers Ltd.

Downes, S. (2005). E-Learning 2.0. *C-Publications in Trade Journals*. Retrieved February 2010 from http://74.125.155.132/scholar?q=cache:LvgWO0I4wIAJ:scholar.google.com/+student+blogging&hl=en&as_sdt=8000000000.

ECAR (2004). *ECAR study of students and information technology, 2005: Convenience, connection, control, and learning*. ECAR Research Study 6. Retrieved January 2010 from www.educause.edu/ers0506.

Falchikov, N., & Goldfinch, J. (2000). Student peer assessment in higher education: A meta-analysis comparing peer and teacher marks. *Review of Educational Research, 70*(3), 287–322.

Fellner, T., & Apple, M. (2006). Developing writing fluency and lexical complexity with blogs. *JALT CALL Journal, 2*(1), 15–26.

Fountain, R. (2005). Wiki pedagogy. *Dossiers technopédagogiques*. Retrieved online from http://profetic.org/dossiers/article.php3?id_article=969

Fulton, K. (1998). *A research study: A framework for considering technology's effectiveness*. Indianapolis, IN: Indiana Department of Education. Retrieved December 2009 from http://ideanet.doe.state.in.us/olr/pdf/appresearchkful.pdf.

Gardner, H. (1993). *Frames of mind: The theory of multiple intelligences*. New York: Perseus Books.

Hmelo-Silver, C. (2004). Problem-based learning: What and how do students learn? *Educational Psychology Review, 16*(3), 235–266.

Ito, M., Baumer, S., Bittanti, M., Boyd, D., Cody, R., Herr-Stephenson, B., . . . Yardi, S. (2009). *Hanging out, messing around, and geeking out: Kids living and learning with new media*. Cambridge, MA: MIT Press.

Levin, D., & Arafeh, S. (2002). *The digital disconnect: The widening gap between Internet-savvy students and their schools*. Washington, DC: American Institutes for Research. Retrieved December 2009 from www.pewinternet.org/pdfs/PIP_Schools_Internet_Report.pdf.

Mayer, R. (2003). Elements of a science of e-learning. *Journal of Educational Computing Research, 29*(3), 297–313.

Mayo, M. (2009). Video games: A route to large-scale STEM education. *Science Magazine, 323*, 79–82.

McKay, E. (1999). An investigation of text-based instructional materials enhanced with graphics. *Educational Psychology, 19*(3), 323–335.

Moore, B. (2010). The Myth Behind Multitasking. *The Michigan Journal*. Retrieved from http://michiganjournal.org/

Moreno, R., & Mayer, R. (2007). Interactive multimodal learning environments. *Educational Psychology Review, 19*, 309–326.

Moreno, R., & Valdez, A. (2005). Cognitive load and learning effects of having students organize pictures and words in multimedia environments: The role of student interactivity and feedback. *Educational Technology Research and Development, 53*(3), 35–45.

Nilson, L. (2003). Improving student peer feedback. *College Teaching, 51*, 18–26.

National School Board Association (NSBA). (2007). *Creating and connecting: Research and guidelines on online social and educational networking*. Retrieved February 2010 from www.nsba.org/site/docs/41400/41340.pdf.

Peck, K., & Dorricott, D. (1994). Why use technology? *Educational Leadership, 51*(7), 11–14.

Prensky, Marc. (2001). *Digital natives, digital immigrants*. Retrieved December 2009 from www.marcprensky.com/writing/.

Richardson, W. (2009). *Blogs, wikis, podcasts, and other powerful web tools for classrooms*. Thousand Oaks, CA: Corwin Press.

Schacter, J., Chung, G., & Dorr, A. (1998). Children's internet searching on complex problems: Performance and process analysis. *Journal of the American Society for Information Science, 49*(9), 840–849.

Second Life. (2013). Retrieved from Wiki.secondlife.com.

Tobin, D. (1998). *Building your personal learning network*. Retrieved from www.tobincls.com/learningnetwork.htm.

Vygotsky, L. S. (1962). *Thought and language*. Cambridge, MA: MIT Press. (Original work published in 1934.)

Wallis, C. (2006). The multitasking generation. *Time Magazine*. Retrieved February 2010 from http://74.125.155.132/scholar?q=cache:V1bRw8n4rc0J:scholar.google.com/+student+multitasking&hl=en&as_sdt=800000000000.

Weir, L. (2008). Research review: Multimodal learning through media. *Edutopia*. Retrieved February 2010 from www.edutopia.org/multimodal-learning-teaching-methods-media.